Skiing In New Jersey?

By: Elizabeth Holste

Skiing In New Jersey?
© 2005, Elizabeth Holste

All rights reserved.

No part of this book may be reproduced, stored in a retrieval system, or transmitted by any means, mechanical, photocopying, recording, scanning or otherwise without the express written permission of the author.

All efforts were taken to contact the original photographers for their permission to use pictures in this book that are not part of the author's collection.

Many of these old ski hills are now on private property. Please respect the owners' privacy and do not trespass.

ISBN: 978-1-4116-6037-3

1st Edition

Elizabeth Holste
holsteliz@hotmail.com

DEDICATION

This book is dedicated to both sets of my grandparents. They bought bungalos in Highland Lakes, New Jersey during the 1960s and I have many happy memories of spending summers and winters there while I was growing up. There are also many great memories of skiing down their neighbors properties and down the snow covered roads of Highland Lakes. Those were my first ski slopes.

This is also dedicated to my parents and my friends who taught me and my sister how to ski. I will always have happy memories of the many hours of fun on the ski slopes learning how to ski.

To my sister Debbie and my brother-in-law Marty thank you for blessing me with my two nephews, Patrick and Jack, to pass my love of skiing on to. I look forward to teaching them how to ski.

Everyone should pass down their memories of skiing in New Jersey or anywhere else to their children and grandchildren. Skiing in New Jersey is something that should not be missed!

Thank you to everyone who helped with my research. I feel honored that I was still able to talk to many of the people who owned these ski hills and to some of the people who remembered skiing at them.

Elizabeth Holste

FOREWORD

Liz takes you back in time to the birth of skiing in one of the most unlikely winter sports states in the country - New Jersey.

Her book honors the spirit of the Europeans who brought their inbred passion for snow and the great outdoors to these shores. The spirit of these pioneers of skiing, described in this book is still alive in those of us who have been lucky enough to reap the rewards of their incredible journey.

Donna Weinbrecht
'92 Olympic Gold Medalist - Freestyle Mogul Skiing

TABLE OF CONTENTS

CHAPTER 1 - A FAST LOOK BACK AT SKIING	9
CHAPTER 2 - LEARNING HOW TO SKI	13
CHAPTER 3 - NOVELTIES AND NEW ALTERNATIVES	21
CHAPTER 4 - ROPE TOWS TO CHAIRLIFTS	23
CHAPTER 5 - SKI TRAINS	25
CHAPTER 6 - NEW JERSEY'S SKI HISTORY	27
CHAPTER 7 - NEW JERSEY'S SKI AREAS	47
CHAPTER 8 - ARROWHEAD	53
CHAPTER 9 - BELLE MOUNTAIN	57
CHAPTER 10 - BERTHIAUME'S	59
CHAPTER 11 – CAMP MIDVALE	61
CHAPTER 12 – CAMPGAW MOUNTAIN	65
CHAPTER 13 – CRAIGMEUR	67
CHAPTER 14 – GALLOPING HILL	73
CHAPTER 15 – GREAT GORGE SKI AREAS	75
CHAPTER 16 – HIDDEN VALLEY	81
CHAPTER 17 – HIGH POINT SKI CENTER	83
CHAPTER 18 – HOLIDAY LAKE	87
CHAPTER 19 – HOLLY MOUNTAIN	91
CHAPTER 20 – HOLMDEL SKI AREA	95
CHAPTER 21 – IDLEBRAE INN	97
CHAPTER 22 – JUGTOWN MOUNTAIN	99
CHAPTER 23 – LAKE TELEMARK SKI JUMPS	103
CHAPTER 24 – MORGAN FARM SKI HILL	107
CHAPTER 25 – MOUNT BETHEL	109
CHAPTER 26 – MOUNTAIN CREEK	115
CHAPTER 27 – NEWTON SKI TOW	119
CHAPTER 28 – NORTH JERSEY COUNTRY CLUB – SKI JUMP	123
CHAPTER 29 – PEAPACK	125
CHAPTER 30 – PINE NEEDLE SLOPE	129
CHAPTER 31 – ROCK VIEW HOTEL	131
CHAPTER 32 – SKI MOUNTAIN	133
CHAPTER 33 – SNOW BOWL	137
CHAPTER 34 – SUCCASUNNA SKI AREA	141
CHAPTER 35 – SUSSEX SKI TOW	143
CHAPTER 36 – THOMPSON PARK	145
CHAPTER 37 – THUNDER MOUNTAIN	147
CHAPTER 38 – VERNON SKI TOW	151
CHAPTER 39 – VERNON VALLEY	157
CHAPTER 40 – PROPOSED SKI AREAS	161
CHAPTER 41 – THE FUTURE	163
REFERENCES	167

CHAPTER 1

A FAST LOOK BACK AT SKIING HISTORY

The history of skiing goes all the way back to around 7,000 and 5,000 BC. Some of the first remnants of ski equipment were found high in the mountains of Norway. The Native Americans also used skis as a means of transportation and to hunt during the winter seasons.

Beginning in 1887, Michigan's Ishpeming Ski Club is one of the oldest ski clubs in the United States. They were also responsible for starting the National Ski Association in 1905. We know it better today as the U.S. Ski and Snowboard Association.

The first wood skis had very crude bindings that were made out of leather straps. The straps were used to tie your short leather ski boots on to the long wood skis you were going to use to ski down the slopes.

One of the first ski factories in the United States opened in St. Paul, Minnesota in 1911. It was originally called C.A. Lund. Later they became known as the Northland Ski Company who were one of the early leaders in ski equipment.

Skis back then were basically just long wood planks that were about 8 feet or longer. You couldn't really turn the skis that you were using back then, so skiing downhill was basically just pointing your skis straight and taking off down the hill. Amazingly there are also still some people who do that today. Brand names for skis like Lund, Northland and Strand were popular at that time.

Cable bindings that looked like bear traps replaced the crude leather straps that were originally used to secure your boots to your skis. Cable bindings and new front and rear boot release systems were introduced to the market after that. Names like Cubco and Spademan were popular early brand names. Today names like Atomic, Look, Marker, Nordica, Rossignol and Tyrolia are the most popular ones.

Ski boots have also come a long way from those old short leather boots with laces. Today's ski boots are much thicker, made out of various composites, are higher, warmer and they better protect a skier's foot. Names like Atomic, Lange, Nordica and Tecnica are popular today.

A FAST LOOK BACK AT SKI HISTORY

The length of skis started to decrease and new composites of wood, steel and fiberglass were being introduced. Professional skiers on the World Cup circuit are now racing on skis that are only about 160cm long. Atomic, Dynastar, Fischer, Rossignol and Volkl are the favorites of today's top men and women ski racers.

A copy of a poster I found showed that the Barnum and Bailey Circus had ski jumping as part of their shows in 1907. "The Flying Norseman", Carl Howelsen, was one of their famous performers. "The Max-Air Blizzard Battalion" still performs amazing ski jumping feats during today's Barnum and Bailey Circus shows.

In the 1920s there already were several small ski resorts in the United States where people could learn how to ski. Most of the skiing back then was cross-country.

There was also a sport called "ski-joring" where you hooked up ropes to a horse and skied behind it. It sounds like it was pretty similar to water skiing. People also went ski-joring on their skis by tying a rope to the back of an old car or truck. I know some people that still try that today.

In the early days of skiing you were probably on a pair of long wooden skis and maybe had one long ski pole to hold on to. That is if you used any ski poles at all. The long ski pole was dragged behind you to help steer and control your speed while taking your run down the slopes. Today little kids are also learning how to ski without using any ski poles. Learning this way seems to help them with being able to find their center of balance.

Most ski history books said in 1932 the first rope tow was developed by Gerhard Mueller. He was an avid skier and a Swiss engineer. The first rope tow at a ski area in North America was in Canada at Foster's Hill. In 1934, the first rope tow in the United States was at Gilbert's Hill in Woodstock, Vermont.

Many more innovations to skis, boots and bindings were made over the years. In the early days, major department stores like Bamberger's, Bloomingdale's, Gimbel's, Sears and Wanamaker's all sold ski equipment in their catalogs and in their stores. Now there are special winter sports shops almost anywhere you go.

A FAST LOOK BACK AT SKI HISTORY

Courtesy of Friends of High Point State Park

THE CIVILIAN CONSERVATION CORPS

Because of the depression, jobs were very hard to come by. The Civilian Conservation Corps was a depression era organization started by President Franklin D. Roosevelt. Young men joined the Civilian Conservation Corps and made about $30 a month. $25 of that money was sent home to their families.

The men in the CCC were responsible for building most of the early State Parks and several of the first ski resorts in the United States. Some of the first ski trails that the CCC men cut were the Bruce and the Toll Road on Mount Mansfield in Vermont. That area would later become known as the Stowe ski area. The CCC also built some of the base lodges, visitor's centers and other amenities at the nation's State Parks.

Almost every state had CCC camps. The camps were run under the direction of the War Department. Unfortunately the idea of the Civilian Conservation Corps started coming to an end during World War II.

A FAST LOOK BACK AT SKI HISTORY

THE 10TH MOUNTAIN DIVISION

During World War II some men joined the famous 10th Mountain Division and trained at special camps in Colorado and Washington. This elite group's main mission during the war was to cross the snow-covered mountains and invade Italy without being discovered. After World War II ended some of the men who were part of the 10th Mountain Division were also responsible for starting some of the ski areas and also becoming ski instructors at them.

I was extremely fortunate to be able to talk to some of these wonderful men while doing my research. They had incredible stories of what it was like to be in the 10th Mountain Division and also how they started some of the first ski resorts. The 10th Mountain Division unfortunately continues its long tradition of being an effective fighting force during some of today's wars. In November 2003, the Vermont Ski Museum inducted many Vermont residents, living and deceased, who were members of the 10th Mountain Division into its Ski Hall of Fame. Two of the living members included Erling Omland and Arnie Kirbach, Sr. originally from the Watchung Ski Club.

10th Mountain Division shoulder patch
Author's collection

CHAPTER 2

LEARNING HOW TO SKI

Author skiing in Highland Lakes, NJ © 1965

Where did you first learn how to ski? Maybe it was at one of New Jersey's ski areas! Can you remember the first time you strapped on a pair of skis and schussed down a mountain? A lot of my friends remembered learning how to ski on a hill in their own back yard or on some other small slope or snow covered road nearby.

Was your first terrifying run down a real ski slope? Do you have memories of someone leaving you at the top of a steep looking slope with no way to get down?

One of my first experiences at a New Jersey ski area was at the Great Gorge South ski area on the Kamikazee slope. I was with a friend that told me it would be really easy for me to learn how to ski. She took me right to the top of the mountain on my first run and then took off down the slope leaving me there. She knew how to ski. I didn't. I was left standing there all alone trying to figure out what to do first – beat her up for leaving me there or try to figure out how to get down to the bottom on my own. It took quite a long time, but I did make it down that first run all by myself.

LEARNING HOW TO SKI

After talking to some of my friends, many of them described how they snow plowed all the way down the mountain on their first runs and being scared to death. A few more tries and they said they were snow plowing down the steepest slopes at blinding speeds.

When kids took their first lessons back in the 1950s and 1960s they were being instructed to make turns that were called Stem Christiana's or Stem Christies, They were also learning how to stop by making what was known as a snow plow or hockey stop. Today kids are learning by making things called Pizza Wedges to stop or slow down.

Your next step was to join a local ski club, then a ski racing team and really speed down the slopes. When ski racing you had the opportunity to be timed to see how fast you could make it down the course. If you were really fast you won a pin or some kind of medal.

Northland wood skis – Courtesy of Doug Kiovsky

LEARNING HOW TO SKI

What was the name of your first pair of skis? How about the name of your first pair of ski boots? Was your first pair of skis made by the Northland Ski Company? Do names like R.H. Macys, Splitkein, Head, Fischer or Rossignol also sound familiar?

If you are over 40 years old, your first pair of skis most likely were just long wood planks with a leather strap used to tie your boots on to the skis. Those first pair of skis probably didn't have metal edges either. If they did, they were sections of thin metal strips that were screwed into the bottom of the skis.

How about your first pair of bindings? Who were they made by? Were they just crude leather straps, or did you have the famous Cubco bindings on your skis? How about names like Spademan, Spaulding, Marker or Tyrolia? They were also popular names in the early days of ski bindings.

Did Bass, Henke, Lange, San Marco or Scott make your first pair of ski boots? Do you remember them having leather shoe laces? Or did they have small metal buckles on them?

Ski technology has also come along way since those early days. Names like Northland, Splitkein and Head were the first familiar ones. Today names like Atomic, Dynastar, K2, Salomon, Rossignol, and Volkl are popular.

Technology began changing quickly. Better metal edges and new bindings as well as new composites of wood, steel and fiberglass were also being introduced to the ski market.

Think back...Did you borrow your first set of ski equipment from everyone that you knew? Did you buy it through a Sears catalog, or at a local ski swap, or a garage sale? Whoever you got it from had already used it for many years before you did. When you got older and had more money you were able to start buying new ski equipment and better ski clothes.

When you started getting into ski racing, you bought a skin tight race suit (just like the ones the pros wear), some protective gear and a helmet. You also bought skis that were made especially for ski racing. And you learned how to wax your racing skis for the different snow conditions. When you first started skiing do you ever remember waxing your skis at all?

LEARNING HOW TO SKI

Who remembers skiing in just jeans and a sweater? Some people probably didn't even wear thermal underwear. Believe it or not, when I go skiing today, I still see people doing that. I guess they are first time skiers, just like we were many years ago.

The people I talked to all had stories of what their first ski equipment was like. It was pretty interesting to think about the equipment we all started on and what we are skiing and snowboarding on now. What a change! I don't know if I could ever go back to using that old equipment. Could you? The new skis and books make skiing so much fun that just about anyone can learn how to ski in a few days.

Today's World Cup and Olympic ski racers are using shaped skis that are only about 5 or 6 feet long!

Believe it or not, major department stores like Bamberger's, Gimbel's, Sears and Wanamaker's all sold ski equipment in their stores and catalogs. Ads in some of the 1930s newspapers showed that the price of skis with leather bindings ranged from $4 to around $50 for a really good pair of wood skis. Today the price of skis, boots and bindings can be as high as $1,000 or more.

A lot of towns had little ski hills in their town or county parks. Some even used hills on the local golf courses. They weren't really ski areas, but many people still talk about learning how to ski on them. Some people even hooked up very crude rope tows on their own property so they could have their own private ski hill.

There were many little ski areas all over New Jersey in the early days. In the 1960s the state's ski industry really started expanding. At one time there were over 20 different ski areas in the state. Unfortunately almost all of them closed down over the years. They are only remembered now by the people who ran them or the people who skied at them.

As I mentioned, some of the golf courses also had small ski runs. The Galloping Hill Golf Course in Kenilworth had a 100 foot vertical slope. Galloping Hill also had two steel toboggan runs in the early days. Rocco's Villa Sunset at Lake Susquehanna had some ski runs. There is a listing from 1958 that said the old Succasunna golf course also had a few ski runs, rope tows and a ski jump.

LEARNING HOW TO SKI

Many county parks like the South Mountain Reservation and the Watchung Reservation also had slopes for skiing, tobogganing and sledding. Of course cross-country, better known as Nordic skiing, is also extremely popular in the state. The cross-country ski areas in New Jersey are too numerous to mention. Practically and farm field, state or county park, golf course, hiking or biking trails, or old railroad beds can be used by the cross-country skiers.

MIGHTY MOUNT MUNSTERER

A father's day article in a past issue of SKI magazine tells the story of another small private family owned ski slope called Mighty Mount Munsterer.

A local skier at Mighty Mount Munsterer – Courtesy of Jerry Munsterer © 2005

LEARNING HOW TO SKI

The SKI magazine story was written by one of the daughters in the family. She said that lots of her friends were jealous when she came to school with big smiles on her face at the start of the day.

After a small local ski area in Mansfield Township closed down, this family bought one of the rope tows and installed it on their property. The kids in the family thought it was pretty cool to have their own ski hill. In the winter they even woke up early enough to get a few runs in before leaving for school.

During some winters private ski races have even been held on Mighty Mount Munsterer. Family members and friends participated in the events. They set up slalom gates, had gate keepers and even had some timing officials just like you would have on a real race course.

Skiers on the slopes of Mighty Mount Munsterer – Courtesy of Jerry Munsterer

LEARNING HOW TO SKI

SCUDDER'S HILL

A letter I received from Mr. Richard B. Scudder said that he powered his private rope tow with engines from lawn mowers. Unfortunately there was no snow making at Scudder's Hill. The family used their private ski slope from around 1957 through the 1960s.

The Scudder family also has an interesting background in New Jersey history. They were the owners of the Newark Evening News newspaper that coincidentally ran a lot of advertisements, articles and pictures of various skiing events. The Newark Evening News also reported on the New Jersey Ski Council's Annual State Race, as well as reporting some unique skiing events such as the indoor "ski slides" in the Bamberger's Department stores.

Wallace Scudder started the Newark News in 1883. Richard co-owned the paper and was the publisher before it was sold in 1970 to the Media General Company. Richard's brother, Edward W. Scudder who was the co-owner and President of the Newark News passed away at the age of 91 on December 5, 2003.

Over the last few years the Scudder family has donated close to 100 acres of their property to the Monmouth County Parks Commission for preservation. Richard Scudder has also served as a Trustee on the commission. Another relative of Richard's also had his own ski hill nearby. It is reported that he also used an old lawn mower engine to run his rope tow.

Scudder's ski hill - Author's Collection

LEARNING HOW TO SKI

Scudder's ski hill – Author's collection

Scudder's ski hill – Author's collection

CHAPTER 3

NOVELTIES AND NEW ALTERNATIVES

After the snow melts skiers get bored in the off season and are always looking for new ways to keep skiing all year long. In England and Japan there are even some places where you can ski indoors on man made slopes. The slope isn't long, but for anyone that can't do without skiing, it's a quick fix.

THE PINE NEEDLE SLOPE

Several newspaper reports I read said the ski hill at the "Rustic R Ranch" was only about 900 feet long. During the late 1930s and early 1940s people skied on a hill that had layers of pine needles on it.

INDOOR SKI SLIDES

In the 1930s some major department stores in Newark and New York City set up short slopes inside their stores so that their customers could try out the ski equipment they were buying. Several newspaper articles said the short slopes were covered with borax soap crystals. Some of the department stores that had these unique indoor ski slopes were Bamberger's, Saks Fifth Avenue and Wanamaker's.

Recently there has been a proposal that includes building an indoor ski slope at a new sports and recreation complex planned for the Meadowlands area in Rutherford. Pretty soon you could be skiing in New Jersey all year long.

GRASS SLOPES

Some of New Jersey's ski areas offered a short-lived sport called Grass Skiing during the summer seasons of the 1970s and 1980s. All you needed were a pair of roller skis and you could take runs down the same trails you skied on during the winter. It was a good idea to make sure you had a box of band aids with you, because falling on the grass and rocks was a lot worse than falling on the snow covered slopes.

SKI MATS

Ski mats can almost simulate the feeling on being on a real ski slope. They are made out of plastic and are similar to the small plastic type grass mats you use in front of your doorstep to wipe your feet on before going into your house. Skis slide pretty well on these mats, and even better – you don't need any snow.

NOVELTIES AND NEW ALTERNATIVES

Some ski areas also used these to cover their slopes before it snows. They seemed to help the snow last longer and they also protected people from the rocks and tree stumps that might still be on the ski slopes. In the winter before the snow season, some ski areas also used ski mats to give early season ski lessons.

OTHER WEIRD SKI STUFF

Something new that has come along in the last few years is Mountain Boarding. It is very similar to snowboarding and skateboarding. Instead of having a flat bottom, you stand on a board and strap your feet into it, just like you would on a snowboard. The Mountain Board has four wheels attached to the bottom. The tires on it are made out of hard rubber. You can stand on it and take off down any hill or clear trail.

People are also skiing on short little skis known as Snow Blades. Some of them are not much longer than the length of your ski boots. These are used on the same trails that everyone skis and snowboards on.

Believe it or not, if you really can't wait to ski, there are even some places in the United States where you can ski on sand hills.

Lots of skiing novelties have surfaced over the years. Who knows how long they will last or what will be next?

CHAPTER 4

ROPE TOWS TO CHAIR LIFTS

Many reports show that one of the first rope tows in the United States was built on Gilbert's Hill in Woodstock, Vermont in 1934.
Records show that the first rope tows in New Jersey were at the High Point ski area and the Craigmeur ski area in the late 1930s.

The first rope tows were very ingenious creations built by the owners or operators of the ski hills. Car engines were used to run the first rope tows. Some of these first speedy tows were made with part from Chevrolet, Ford and Oldsmobile cars from the late 1920s and early 1930s. Some ski areas even used lawn mower engines or tractor engines to power their rope tows.

Old Roebling ad from an issue of the American Ski Annual

ROPE TOWS TO CHAIR LIFTS

A rope tow is a continuous length of rope or cable run through a pulley system that is attached to tall poles or trees. The tows pull skiers back up to the top of the slope so they can take another run. Some of the early ones ran at pretty high speeds. The Roebling Company was a wire cable company that also built some of the first tows. There were lots of funny accidents when people would forget to let go of the rope when they fell.

OTHER LIFTS

Other types of lifts were soon developed after rope tows. They included T-Bars, J-Bars, pomas, chair lifts and gondolas. Some of the chair lifts started out as single chairs and then were made into doubles, triples and quads. At some ski areas in the United States there are even "six pack" chairs. That means that six people can go up a ski lift chair at one time.

The first chair lifts at many of New Jersey's ski areas were Borvig lifts. Some ski areas started with single chair lifts. In later years came doubles, triples and quads. Today there is even a gondola at one of New Jersey's ski areas.

Author's collection

Courtesy of Ted Hine © 1947

CHAPTER 5

SKI TRAINS

In the 1930s some railroad companies began running special Winter Ski Trains or Snow Trains out to the new ski resorts. Brochures about some of them were also handed out on the trains as well as in some of Newark and New York City's major department stores.

Stores like Bamberger's, Saks Fifth Avenue and Wanamaker's also sponsored winter ski events and indoor ski shows that were held in places like the Madison Square Garden and the New York Coliseum.

During the winter there were special ski trains that ran to New Jersey, New York, Pennsylvania, Vemont, Massachusetts and other northeastern state's ski areas for the weekends and special holidays like Christmas or New Year's Eve.

The ski trains would leave in the early morning on Friday or Saturday and drop you at your skiing destination for the weekend. They picked you up again on Sunday and brought you back home.

Most of the Ski Trains had coach cars, sleeping and dining cars and also special cars where you could also get touch ups or repairs on your ski equipment while you were traveling. Some of them even sold new ski equipment and clothing before you arrived at your destination.

The Erie Railroad has a Ski Train that went from Newark, New Jersey to Port Jervis, New York in 1936. The Bamberger's Department Store and other well-known department stores sponsored some of the Snow Trains.

Some 1930s newspaper articles reported that from New York City you could be at the High Point State Park in Sussex, New Jersey in about two hours. Skiers arrived at the Port Jervis train station and then were taken by a bus up to the High Point State Park's ski center.

There was another Erie Snow Train in the 1940s that ran to the Midvale train station where skiers were then brought to the Camp Midvale Ski Center in Ringwood.

Another Snow Train ran to the Newfoundland train station where skiers were brought to the Craigmeur ski area. There were others that ran out towards the Jugtown Mountain ski area and the Peapack ski area.

SKI TRAINS

In the 1970s there was a Susquehanna Snow Train that ran out to the Great Gorge South ski area in Vernon. This was really convenient because the tracks ran right behind the back of the Great Gorge South's parking lot. A small train stop was set up there that made it convenient for skiers to get to the slopes.

Unfortunately the novelty of Ski Trains died out and that made it difficult for many skiers to get to the ski slopes in New Jersey.

In 2000 the Mountain Creek ski area partnered up with New Jersey Transit to run special ski buses out to the ski area from Port Authority in New York City. As of 2003, those ski buses are still running. There are also rumors that the train service to the area could possibly be restarted.

Courtesy of Friends of High Point State Park © 1936

CHAPTER 6

NEW JERSEY'S SKIING HISTORY

Is your favorite ski area in New Jersey still open? You may not believe it but skiing in New Jersey has a long history. Were you part of it?

Anyone that has skied in New Jersey says: "If you can ski here, you can ski anywhere!" Our slopes were known to be some of the iciest ones around.

Many people wouldn't even think of New Jersey when they were deciding where they wanted to go skiing. The "big" ski areas are in New York State, Pennsylvania, and farther north. Some people would laugh at you when you told them you went skiing in New Jersey. They would say: "Skiing in New Jersey? Where? There's no skiing in that state!"

Many skiers already began exploring the various mountain regions in New Jersey in the early 1900s to see where they might be able to set up a ski hill. Even at that time, some of the farm hills and fields were being developed for summer and winter recreation and vacation areas.

In the winter most farmers did nothing with the hills and fields on their farms, so they allowed some of them to be used for sledding and skiing. They also found out pretty fast that they could make some extra money by doing that.

In the 1920s and 1930s skiing was nothing like it is today. Back then most of the skiing was basically cross-country. Alpine skiing was basically just pointing your long wood skis straight down the hill and taking your run. The long wood skis were extremely hard to turn at first. Once you skied down a slope and wanted to take another run, you had to walk back up to the top.

Rope tows began sprouting up all over in New Jersey's early ski history. Some people figured out how to build crude rope tows from car engines to get skiers back to the top of the slopes without them having to walk back up to take their next runs. Who knew that Ford, Chrysler and Oldsmobile made some of the first rope tows! Some of those first rope tows were reported to be pretty fast too.

Many reports said that you had a quicker ride up the hill than you did when you skied down. A few of the early rope tows were so quick that they were also known to rip through skier's gloves and some of their ski clothes.

NEW JERSEY'S SKI HISTORY

People watching the skiers also had some pretty good laughs when the skiers would forget to let go of the rope tow after they fell and were then dragged on the ground.

I found some old reports that said the first recorded ski hill in New Jersey was on a farmer's field between Sussex and High Point State Park. The exact location unfortunately was not given. However, there are remnants of several old rope tows on various farm fields and hills in that area. One of them could be where skiing first started in New Jersey. The Craigmeur ski area in Newfoundland became the first official ski area in the state during the winter of 1936 / 1937.

I spoke to some people who remembered an old ski hill in the 1940s that was called the Sussex Ski Tow. Others remembered it as Spreen's Ski Tow. This ski hill was located off Route 23 near the old Upsala College Wirths Campus in Lewisburg.

Some local skiers remembered another ski hill called the "Newton Ski Tow". This one was located on directly across from where the Sussex County Community College stands today.

Local radio stations like WOR gave daily snow reports in the late 1960s and 1970s. The WOR radio station was started in a corner of the sporting goods department of the Bamberger's store in Newark.

Newspapers like the Newark Evening News, the New York Times and the Star-Ledger all ran various articles and advertisements about skiing.

In the late 1960s there was a group formed that was called the Ski 23 Association. It was just like New Hampshire's Ski 93 Association. It consisted of the Craigmeur ski area in Newfoundland, Snow Bowl in Milton, and Great Gorge in McAfee.

Many of the owners and operators of the ski areas in New Jersey also became part of an organization called the New Jersey Ski Areas Association. This organization helped draft some of the early legislation on how the state's ski areas should operate and how they were able to handle legal disputes.

NEW JERSEY'S SKI HISTORY

ADULT RACING PROGRAMS

Adults can participate in many different racing leagues during the winter. There are programs ranging from NASTAR, company leagues, bar leagues as well as the New Jersey Ski Council races that are hosted against many of the ski clubs in the state. If you ever wanted to see what ski racing is like, there are plenty of opportunities to try it.

NEW JERSEY SKI RACING ASSOCIATION

John Pier formed the New Jersey Ski Racing Association (NJSRA) in 1980. It was developed to offer a more structured racing program than was available through the New Jersey Ski Council. It is a non-profit, volunteer organization.

Greg Pier is the current President of the organization and manages a fantastic program that is run out of the Campgaw, Hidden Valley and Mountain Creek ski areas. Members of the NJSRA include the racers, coaches, gate keepers, and parents of the racers. The New Jersey Ski Racing Association hosts sanctioned United States Ski Association (USSA) and FIS ski and snowboard races at many different resorts. Children of all different ages participate in these races.

Many notable skiers have come out of the NJSRA program. A number of them went on to participate in college, World Cup and Olympic ski races. Some of them include:

Wanda Arendarski	Jr. III Eastern Junior Olympic Champion
Jamie Kurlander	U.S. Ski Team, World Cup/Pro Circuit
Robert McGraw	Plymouth State College
Jerry Munsterer	St. Lawrence University
Molly Munsterer	Notre Dame
Greg Pier	University of Maine/NJSRA President/St. Lawrence University Head Ski Coach, USSA Children's Committee Chairman – Eastern Division

NEW JERSEY'S SKI HISTORY

John Pier	Williams College/1st Team All American
Todd Schneider	U.S. Ski Team
Donna Weinbrecht	World Cup Pro & 1992 US Olympic Mogul Champ
Joy Weinbrecht	Plymouth State College

Many of New Jersey's elementary, high schools and colleges also have ski racing programs. We can be proud that some of New Jersey's ski areas have been the training ground for many amateur and even a few professional ski racers and snowboarders.

ART TOKLE, Sr.

Art's family moved to Lake Telemark, New Jersey and continued his family's long history in the sport of ski jumping. His uncle, Torger Tokle, held the jump record at Bear Mountain, New York that was never broken. Art Tokle competed in the 1952 and 1960 Winter Olympics.

He was one of the people who helped find the locations and build the two ski jumps that were located in Lake Telemark. He later helped build other ski jumps at the Craigmeur and Great Gorge ski areas.

Art also participated in many ski jumping competitions at Bear Mountain, NY and throughout the United States. After retiring from competing, at the age of 40, he became a coach and trained many other people in the art of ski jumping.

ART TOKLE Jr.

Art Tokle, Jr. grew up in Lake Telemark and spent many hours on the Odin Ski Club's ski jumps. He still lives there with his family. He continues the Tokle family's long history of ski jumping today. As of 2005 he is still listed as the Chairman of the Eastern USSA Ski Jumping Committee.

ELLEN SKAVNES

Ellen also grew up in Lake Telemark. She started skiing when she was 3 years old. Her ski jumping career first began on the Odin Ski Club's jumps. She told me that she was one of the first women ski jumpers on the East Coast during the 1940s and 1950s.

NEW JERSEY'S SKI HISTORY

She also competed on the famous ski jump at Bear Mountain State Park in New York. In February 1957 at a ski jump competition held at Bear Mountain, she was the only woman to compete, and placed 6th out of 12 participants in the 15 to 17 year old juniors group. Her coach was Art Tokle, Sr.

DONNA WEINBRECHT

Author's collection

At the town lines of West Milford there are several large signs congratulating Donna Weinbrecht, the 1992 Olympic Gold Medal winner. Donna Weinbrecht's rise to fame has done more for the sport of women's mogul skiing competitions than any other women who participated in them. Her fame has also done a lot for the recognition of all women ski racers in general.

She was born in Hoboken, New Jersey but lists her hometowns as West Milford, New Jersey and Killington, Vermont.

When I talked with Donna she told me that she started skiing when she was around 7 years old on the slopes of the Hidden Valley ski area in Vernon. In High School she and one of her girlfriends started the West Milford High School ski team.

NEW JERSEY'S SKI HISTORY

Hidden Valley ski pass – courtesy of Donna Weinbrecht

When she was a teenager her family bought a house in Vermont and she started skiing down the famous Outer Limits mogul run at the Killington ski area. Donna told me that when she first started competing in bump contests, she had no real training. Everything she learned in the early days was just by watching other people. Her skiing career seemed to fall into place after High School when the design school she attended unfortunately shut down. When we talked it seemed she happened to be in the right place at the right time and entered the world of mogul competitions.

Outer Limits is one of her most favorite mogul runs on the East Coast. Ms. Weinbrecht has been a participant in many of the Annual Killington Mogul Challenges that are held every April. If you ski at Killington you might find her still crashing the bumps on her favorite trail, or being one of the judges at the annual bump competitions.

Her skiing career includes being a member of the U.S. Ski Team for about 14 years. In the 1980s and 1990s Donna dominated the sport of women's mogul competitions. Most skiers refer to her as the bump queen of the United States.

Donna has also been a spokesperson for the Killington Ski Resort, Rossignol Ski Company, Oakley eyewear and several other well known companies. She has also worked as a commentator for CBS Sports and the Fox Network. Donna currently makes appearances throughout the country on behalf of the U.S. Ski Team.

NEW JERSEY SKI HISTORY

Donna is probably the most famous of New Jersey's Winter Olympians. She helped pave the way for today's breed of extreme free skiers. In 1992 she won the first ever Olympic Gold Medal awarded in Freestyle Moguls in the Olympics in Albertville, France. She is a three time Olympian.

Donna Weinbrecht was inducted into the 2004 class in the United States National Ski Hall of Fame which is located in Ishpeming, Michigan.

Donna's long mogul skiing record includes:

Olympic Gold Medal	1992
World Championships Gold	1991
World Championships Silver	1989 and 1997
World Cup Moguls Title	1990, '91, '92, '94, '96
US National Champion	1988, '89, '90, '91, '92, '94, '96
World Cup Medals	46 Gold, 12 Silver, 12 Bronze

Awards

Finalist for the Women's Sports Foundation's
    "Sportwoman of the Year" – 1996

Winner of Ski Racing Magazine's "Int'l & US Female Freestyle"
    1993 & 1996

Inductee – 2004 class of the United States National Ski Hall of Fame.

JAMIE KURLANDER

Jamie was also a member of the U.S Ski Team. Her father, Jack Kurlander, was one of the original builders of the Great Gorge ski area, where Jamie got her start in ski racing. As a child, Jamie participated in many of the NJSRA ski races before heading out on to the professional ski racing circuit. Jamie was a member of the U.S. Ski Team for many years and also raced in the World Cup, and the Pro Circuit. When she finally retired from slalom ski racing, she was ranked 30th in the world.

Jamie's skiing career includes:

U.S. Ski Team
A Team – 1977 to 1979
B Team – 1975 to 1976, 1980
World Champions Team – 1978

NEW JERSEY SKI HISTORY

DANNY KASS

There are signs at the borders of the town of Vernon that congratulate Danny Kass the 2002 Olympic Silver medal winner. In 2002 Danny became New Jersey's newest Winter Olympic athlete. Reports say that Danny learned how to snowboard at the local ski areas in Vernon. There are also reports that Donna Weinbrecht's brother, Jimmy, taught Danny how to snowboard.

Danny Kass already has several national snowboarding championship titles. He took 1st place at the 2001 Winter X-Games. He won a Silver medal at the 2002 Winter Olympics in Utah.

For a state that is not seriously considered a ski mecca, there are many top amateur ski racers that had their start on the small ski hills of New Jersey. Our state has also produced several Winter Olympians. Incredible for a state that people do not believe has any ski hills.

How many more Olympic champions will there be from New Jersey? Will you be one of them?

SKI JUMPS IN NEW JERSEY

Ski jumping was another winter sport experimented with in New Jersey. There were several ski jumps in our state. One of the first ones was built in 1925.

NEW JERSEY SKI HISTORY

Surprising as it sounds, our state was a haven for ski jumping competitions in the early days. In doing my research I found that ski jumping wasn't only done during the winter. Believe it or not, there are records of jump competitions being held during the summer and the fall seasons. Some were held on crushed ice, plastic sheets and even on a pine needle slope.

Unfortunately all of the ski jumps in New Jersey were taken down years ago. If you do some searching around though, you might be able to still find remnants of a few of them.

SKI JUMPS	LOCATION	OPENED	CLOSED
Craigmeur	Newfoundland	1963	1967
Great Gorge South	McAfee	1968	1970s
High Point Ski Center	Sussex	1936	1960s
North Jersey C.C.	Wayne	1925	1927
Odin Ski Club Jumps	Lake Telemark	1948	1962
Peapack	Peapack	1939	1987
Pine Needle Slope	Swartswood Lake	1939	1940s
Rocco's Villa Sunset	Lake Susquehanna	1940s	1950s
Succasunna Ski Area	Succasunna	1940s	1960s

Ski jump at Great Gorge South - Author's collection

NEW JERSEY'S SKI HISTORY

OTHER SKI JUMPS

Other small ski hills like the one at Rocco's Villa Sunset at Lake Susquehanna and the one at the Succasunna Ski Area also had ski jumps. Unfortunately there is not much information available about these two ski hills. It seems that they only lasted for a few years from the 1940s to the 1950s or 1960s.

One of the most popular ski jumps in the East was just across the border in New York's Bear Mountain State Park. This jump was open from 1928 through 1990. There are some newspaper reports that said more jump competitions were held there than at any other ski jump in the United States.

In the 1950s and 1960s home made ski jumps popped up in anyone's back yard or on some hill that was steep enough to ski down. There were other reports of skiing and jump shows being held inside the New York Coliseum and the Madison Square Garden also in New York during the 1930s.

One of the Winter sports shows at the Madison Square Garden had a long ski jump that ran from the top of the arena down to the floor. Crushed ice was put on the slope for the professional ski shows that were part of the festivals.

The Barnum and Bailey Circus also had amazing ski jumping feats as part of their shows as early as 1907. Carl Howelsen was one of their top ski jump performers. He was known as "The Flying Dutchman". Barnum and Bailey's web site also says that the Max-Air Blizzard Battalion still performs ski jumping as part of their circus shows. Skiing, snowboarding and ski jumping all have a long history in New Jersey, as well as the rest of the United States.

NEW JERSEY'S SKI HISTORY

THE L. BAMBERGER COMPANY

Louis Bamberger and his family ran a successful chain of department stores under their family name. The Bamberger Company was very involved in promoting the sport of skiing for many years.

In the mid 1930s Bamberger's Department Store was one of the sponsors of winter snow trains that brought skiers from Newark and the surrounding area to the High Point State Park in Sussex. They also ran snow trains to the Pocono Mountains and Hazelton, Pennsylvania.

Skiers going to the High Point State Park would be picked up by a bus from the Port Jervis, New York train station and were brought up to the park.

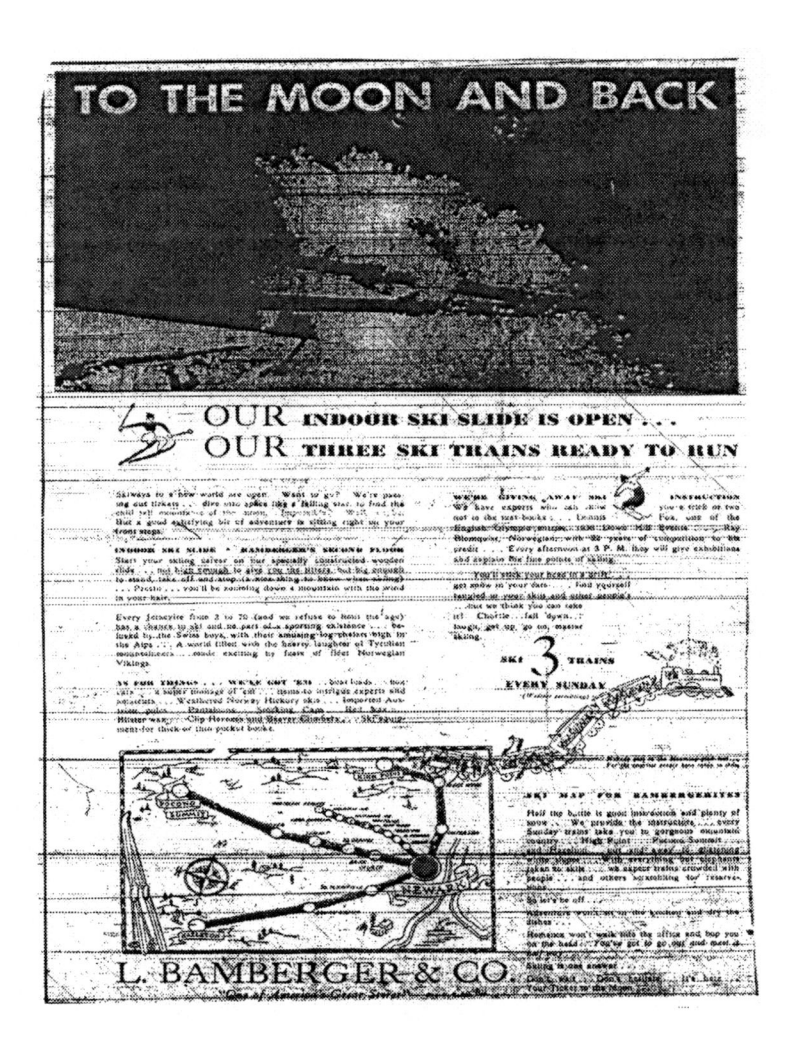

Old Bamberger's advertisement

NEW JERSEY'S SKI HISTORY

In 1937 the L. Bamberger Company built a small ski slope inside their stores so that customers could try out the new ski equipment they were buying. A description of the slope said it was sixty tow feet long and it was about 12 feet wide. It was carpeted and borax soap crystals were used on it to give it the look and feel of real snow. There were even two ski instructors at the store who gave free ski lessons.

In the mid to late 1930s several of the other major department stores also had indoor ski slopes. There were full-page ads for them in the New York Times and several other newspapers.

In the 1940s the Bamberger Company also arranged free ski lessons for anyone that wanted them at the South Mountain Reservation. They also provided ski rental equipment. This was organized by Bamberger's and the Essex County Park Commission.

Bamberger's also sponsored a ski racing trophy in the early 1940s that is still being won today by many of the top New Jersey ski clubs racing teams. The trophy is awarded to the winning team of the New Jersey Ski Council's State Race. Even though it is called the New Jersey State Race, it has been held other northeastern states.

The first year the trophy was awarded to the Snow Chasers from Morristown. The Watchung Ski Club was the second team to win it. New Jersey State Race has been continually run for over 60 years, and the Bamberger Trophy has also been circulating through the various New Jersey ski clubs for over 60 years.

In the 1930s and 1940s Bamberger's would also hold winter sports shows and carnivals inside their stores. Ads for them appeared in the Newark Evening News and the New York Times. These sports shows were held inside their store every year in the beginning of December. The shows were complete with the indoor ski slope an indoor ice skating rink and winter sports fashion shows. Bamberger's continued promoting skiing and other sports for many years.

NEW JERSEY'S SKI HISTORY

COLLINS SKI PRODUCTS

Bergenfield also had a company located there in the 1970s that was involved in the ski industry. Collins Ski Products were the manufacturers of the I-dent-I-Ski locks that many skiers used to protect their skis while they were taking a break in the ski lodge.

Collins lock advertisement

NEW JERSEY'S SKI HISTORY

THE CUBCO BINDING COMPANY

Mitch Cubberley was a graduate of the Stevens Institute. He was interested in mechanical engineering and also loved to ski. In the basement of his house in Belleville around 1948 he started making his own ski bindings. As it grew, the Cubco Binding Company later relocated to a bigger space in Nutley. They made some of the first front and rear binding release systems. From the 1950s throughout the 1970s there were several different versions of Cubco bindings. Cubco also made the first "ski stoppers" (The Cubco Skidder) – better known today as ski brakes. The Cubco Binding Company continued making ski bindings until 1979. I'm sure if you ask around you might find some people that probably still have a pair of Cubco bindings hidden in their basement.

Old Cubco advertisement

NEW JERSEY'S SKI HISTORY

THE GARCIA COMPANY

Gordon Lipe began as a consultant for the Garcia Company and was another one of the early inventors of ski binding release systems. He also developed a system of levers and springs that we now know as the ski brake. The Garcia Company was located in Teaneck. The Gordon Lipe Slider and the Lipe Release Check were the names of the binding release systems sold by company.

The Garcia Company was one of the leaders of manufacturing, importing, and distributing ski products during the 1970s. The Garcia Company was also a distributor of the famous Burt ski bindings. The Lange Company is an affiliate of the Garcia Company and remains one of the most popular ski product companies today.

NEW JERSEY SKI COUNCIL

The New Jersey Ski Council was founded in 1939 to help promote the sport of skiing. Several members who started the Watchung Ski Club also started the New Jersey Ski Council. Erling Omland was listed as one of the New Jersey Ski Council's first presidents.

There have been many different ski clubs that have been part of the New Jersey Ski Council. Club names have included: the Snow Chasers, the Crust Busters, the Watchung Ski Club, the High Life Ski Club and the Garden State Ski Club. The New Jersey Ski Council celebrated its 65th Anniversary in 2004.

One of the benefits for New Jersey's ski clubs for being a member of the council is that they can purchase discount lift tickets to many different ski areas in New Jersey, New York and Vermont.

The council also hosts an extremely popular week night adult ski and snowboard racing league. Many of New Jersey's ski clubs and even a few New York ski clubs have racing teams that compete in this league.

The first weekend in February the council hosts the New Jersey Ski Council State Race. Records show that this race has been an annual event since the 1940s. A trophy is awarded to the winning team. I found an old newspaper article that said the Bamberger Company sponsored the trophy.

NEW JERSEY'S SKI HISTORY

The New Jersey Ski Council hosts a winter kick off Jamboree party in October or November every year. All of New Jersey's ski clubs have booths with their members telling everyone what each club has to offer. At the Jamborees there are also various ski resorts with their own booths and most of them also host raffles where you can win a free lift ticket or maybe even a complete ski trip. Olympic skiers like Billy Kidd, Dianne Roffee Steiner as well as several others have also been guests at many of the New Jersey Ski Council Jamborees.

The Jamborees are a great way for skiers and snow boarders to learn about the different ski clubs in New Jersey. Many New Jersey ski clubs also have their own ski lodges in Vermont or upstate New York.

JOHN A. ROEBLING COMPANY

The Roebling Company was established in Trenton, New Jersey in 1849. It was a very unique company because they built their own housing and a town where their workers could live while they were working for the company. They were one of the first companies to produce wire rope, also known as wire cables. Their wire rope was used in many different applications from bridges and elevators to ski lifts.

The new ski lifts consisted of a wire cable that ran over your head in a continual loop. In the early days J-Bars and T-Bars were attached to them.
In later years single chairs to gondolas were attached to the wire rope.

The new over head lifts began to appear at ski areas all over the world as early as 1934.

One of the first Roebling J-Bar lifts was installed in Switzerland at the Davos ski area that year. The first Roebling T-Bar lifts appeared on the slopes of the Pico ski area in Vermont during 1940.

42

NEW JERSEY'S SKI HISTORY

One of the last Roebling T-Bars reported to be built in the United States was in 1970 at a New Hampshire ski area.

NEW JERSEY'S SKI HISTORY

NEW JERSEY - the 1900s to 2005

1925	Ski jump opens at North Jersey Country Club in Wayne.
1930s	New Jersey's first ski clubs start forming.
1930s	Skiing at Camp Midvale in Ringwood.
1934	President Hoover creates the Civilian Conservation Corps.
1934	Some skiing at High Point State Park.
1935	First Winter Sports Show held inside Madison Square Garden in New York City.
1936	National Ski Patrol is created.
1936	Craigmeur Ski Area opens in Newfoundland.
1937	Skiing at Rock View Hotel in Montague.
1937	Skiing at the Pine Needle Slope in Swartswood Lake.
1939	Peapack ski area opens in Peapack.
1940s	Rocco's Villa Sunset in Lake Susquehanna offers skiing.
1940s	Galloping Hill ski area opens in Kenilworth.
1940s	Skiing at Morgan Farm in Cedar Grove.
1940s	Skiing at Succasunna ski area in Succasunna.
1946	Vernon Ski Tow area opens on Pochuck Mountain in Vernon.
1947	Newton Ski Tow area in Newton opens.
1947	Skiing at Sussex Tow area in Lewisburg.
1948	Gretchen Fraser is the first American woman to win medals in the Winter Olympics.
1948	Cubco Binding Company in Nutley introduces some of the first front and rear ski boot release systems for alpine skis.
1948	The Odin Ski Club forms and their members also build ski jumps in Lake Telemark.
1950s	Snow making equipment is developed and used for the first time at some of the East Coast's new ski areas.
1950s	Skiing at Ringwood's Thunder Mountain.
1952	Andrea Mead Lawrence is the first American woman to win two Gold medals in the Winter Olympics for Giant Slalom.
1955	First snow making equipment is installed at the Craigmeur Ski Area in Newfoundland.
1960	Ski jump competitions are held in November in New York City's Central Park.
1960	Belle Mountain ski area opens in Hopewell Township.
1960s	Holmdel ski area opens in Holmdel.
1960s	Mt. Bethel ski area in Mansfield Township opens.
1961	Skiing at Campgaw Mountain in Mahwah.
1962	Jugtown Mountain ski area in Asbury opens.

NEW JERSEY SKI HISTORY

1964	Billy Kidd and Jim Huega become the first American men to win medals in the Winter Olympics. Billy Kidd won a Silver medal and Jim Huega won a bronze medal.
1964	Arrowhead ski area opens at YMCA Camp Arrowhead in Marlboro.
1964	Thompson Park ski center opens in Jamesburg.
1965	Jack Kurlander and John Fitzgerald open the Great Gorge ski area on Hamburg Mountain in Vernon.
1966	The first World Cup ski races are held.
1966	Ski hills at Holiday Lake in Montague.
1968	Vernon Valley ski area opens in Vernon.
1970s	Skiing at Holly Mountain in Lower Alloways Creek.
1971	Great Gorge North ski area opens in Vernon.
1976	Jack Kurlander opens the Hidden Valley ski area in Vernon.
1992	Donna Weinbrecht wins the first Gold medal for mogul skiing at the Winter Olympics in Albertville, France.
1998	Intrawest buys the Vernon Valley/Great Gorge ski areas in Vernon, and reopens them as a new resort called Mountain Creek.
1998	Craigmeur ski area in Newfoundland closes down.
2002	Danny Kass wins the first Silver medal for snowboarding in the Winter Olympics in Park City, Utah.
2003	Plans are announced to build an indoor ski center at the Xanadu Complex in the Meadowlands area near Rutherford.
2004	Donna Weinbrecht, 1992 Olympics Mogul Champion inducted into the U.S. National Ski Hall of Fame.
2005	The former Craigmeur ski area property is sold to the Morris County Parks Commission to be preserved as open space.

CHAPTER 7

NEW JERSEY SKI AREAS

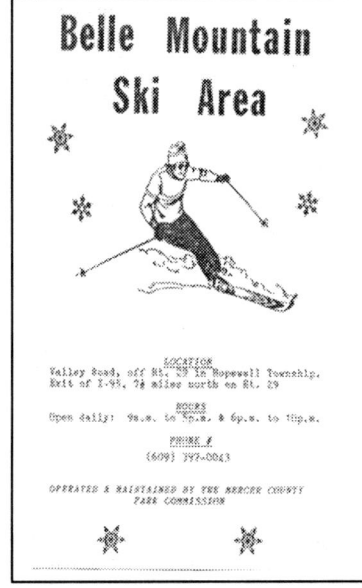

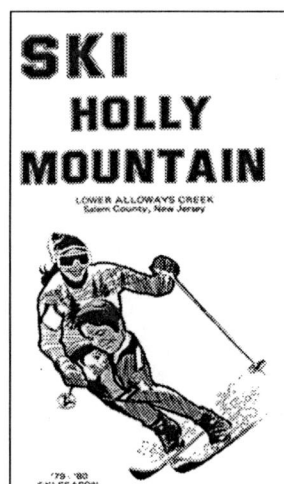

47

NEW JERSEY'S SKI AREAS

SKI PATCHES

48

NEW JERSEY'S SKI AREAS

Before skiing on the "official" ski hills of New Jersey, many people skied on their own back yard hills or local roads that were covered with snow. There were also small ski hills like Rocco's Villa Sunset in Lake Susquehanna near Blairstown and the Idlebrae Inn near Montague.

Lots of people took their first real trips to the slopes in either elementary school or high school. The ski groups were usually run by one of the teachers from the school who also skied. These ski groups are still being run today. However, tour companies are now usually hired to run them.

Most ski clubs or ski groups offered five or six trips to the local ski areas. How many people remember taking those first rides on the school buses to go to the slopes? Some high schools and colleges also have their own ski and snowboard racing teams.

SUSSEX COUNTY SKI AREAS

There were already several small ski areas in the Sussex County area before the Great Gorge South ski area appeared in 1965. Records show that there were several small ski tows on farms and fields here earlier, but unfortunately they didn't have any snowmaking equipment. Because of that they only operated for a few years. From the 1930s throughout the early 1960s the people who owned these ski areas offered skiing basically to share their enjoyment of the sport with other people than to really try to make a profit from their operations.

Towns such as Freedon, High Point, Lewisburg, Montague, Newton, Vernon and Wantage all seem to have records of ski tows being run in those areas. Some of these ski hills used old 1930s Ford Model A car engines to power their rope tows. Many of the early ski hills were not very long or very steep, but they provided hours of fun for the people that skied at them. Ski hills like Berthiaume's - High Point Ski Ways, Holiday Lake, the Newton Ski Tow, the Sussex Ski Tow and the Vernon Ski Tow were some of Sussex County's earliest ski areas.

Lots of farmers opened their fields and hillsides in the winter to anyone who wanted to ski. A man by the name of Gib Roby built several of the ski tows near the Montague area. In years when there was enough natural snow, some of the railroad companies even ran winter sports trains to a few of the Sussex County ski hills.

NEW JERSEY'S SKI AREAS

In the 1960s and 1970s New Jersey's ski resort industry really exploded. Jack Kurlander and John Fitzgerald were the major forces in bringing large scale skiing to the northern part of the state. Four ski areas were built in Vernon during that time. In 1965 Jack Kurlander, John Fitzgerald and several other investors built the Great Gorge ski area. With the invention of T-Bars and chair lifts, longer and steeper ski slopes and larger ski areas could be opened for the public to ski on.

PLAYBOY BUNNIES ON THE SLOPES!

In the 1970s Hugh Heffner built the Playboy Club hotel in Vernon and brought his infamous Playboy bunnies to the ski slopes of northern New Jersey. The new hotel helped bring back a large interest in skiing in the state. Hopes of spotting one of the Playboy bunnies on the slopes also helped.

To enter the grounds of the Playboy Club hotel, you had to have a special key card. The hotel had just about everything you would find at the larger resorts in the northeast or out west. It had hundreds of rooms, conference and banquet rooms, several bars, sidewalk cafés, several restaurants, various shops, a disco, indoor tennis courts, an 18 hole golf course, a gym and an indoor and outdoor swimming pool. Original plans for the hotel also included a gambling casino, however, that unfortunately was never approved.

For many years during the 1970s and early 1980s you could find the Playboy bunnies walking around the hotel serving drinks and dinners. You may have even seen some of them out on the slopes of Vernon's ski resorts. Many celebrities also frequented the hotel by performing there.

In 1984, the Playboy Club hotel was sold to the Americana hotel chain. The hotel was sold several more times over the years to various investors. There are plans to turn it into time share condos.

NEW JERSEY'S SKI AREAS

NEW JERSEY'S LOST SKI AREAS

SKI AREA	LOCATION	OPEN	CLOSED
Arrowhead	Marlboro	1964	1986
Belle Mountain	Hopewell Township	1960	1998
Berthiaume's	Montague	1960	1960s
Camp Midvale	Ringwood	1930s	1970s
Craigmeur	Newfoundland	1937	1998
Galloping Hill	Kenilworth	1940s	1980s
Great Gorge North	Vernon	1971	1997
Great Gorge South	McAfee	1965	1997
High Point Ski Center	High Point State Park	1937	1964
Holiday Lake (golf course)	Montague	1966	1970s
Holiday Lake (pipe line)	Montague	1966	1970s
Holly Mountain	Lower Alloways Creek	1970s	1986
Holmdel Ski Area	Holmdel Township	1960s	1970s
Idlebrae Inn	Montague	1964	1966
Jugtown Mountain	Asbury	1961	1971
Morgan Farm Ski Hill	Cedar Grove	1940s	1960s
Mount Bethel	Mansfield Township	1960s	1970s
Newton Ski Tow	Newton	1947	1951
North Jersey CC Jumps	Wayne	1924	1927
Odin Ski Club Jumps	Lake Telemark	1948	1962
Peapack Ski Area	Peapack	1939	1987
Pine Needle Slope	Swartswood Lake	1939	1940s
Rocco's Villa Sunset	Lake Susquehanna	1940s	1950s
Rock View Hotel	Montague	1937	1960s
Ski Mountain	Pine Hill	1964	1986
Sleepy Hollow Park Camp	Sussex	???	1970s
Snow Bowl	Milton	1962	1973
South Mountain	South Orange	1940s	1980s
Succasunna Ski Hill	Succasunna	1940s	1960s
Sussex Ski Tows	Lewisburg	1947	1950s
Thompson Park Ski Hill	Jamesburg	1964	1980s
Thunder Mountain	Ringwood	1950s	1973
Vernon Ski Tow	Vernon Township	1946	1949
Vernon Valley	Vernon	1968	1997

NEW JERSEY'S OPEN SKI AREAS

Campgaw Mountain	Mahwah	1961	OPEN
Hidden Valley	Vernon	1976	OPEN
Mountain Creek	Vernon	1998	OPEN

NEW JERSEY'S SKI AREAS

Do you remember any other lost ski areas or ski hills in New Jersey that weren't on the list? There could be many more.

Even though most of these ski areas closed many years ago, remnant of some of the old lodges, ski slopes and whatever is left of the rope tows or chair lift equipment can still be seen.

Rusted remains of an old chair lift - Author's Collection

CHAPTER 8

ARROWHEAD SKI AREA
521 County Road 520
Marlboro

Entrance sign for Camp Arrowhead
Author's collection

The YMCA's Camp Arrowhead has been operating since 1958. The camp is still open and has many outdoor activities for families that come there.

The ski area was on a hillside on the 36 acres of the camp. Skiing started there when James Brotherton, Wilbur Van Lenten, Richard Dawson and a small group of men started the Arrowhead Ski Club in 1964. James Brotherton was the first President of the Arrowhead Ski Club. Newspaper reports said that the new ski club cleared the land and began their tow system by hooking it up to an old tractor. It was also reported that the Bell Telephone Company donated several large telephone poles. Some old wheel rims were attached to them to complete the rope tow system. Around 1966 a larger engine was purchased and hooked up to operate the rope tows.

Some of the first ski lessons were given on a straw covered slope at the Arrowhead Ski Area during the 1966. In 1967 plastic mats were bought and then ski lessons could be held on the slopes almost any time during the year. The mats were used for early season ski lessons every year up to 1986 when the ski area closed.

ARROWHEAD SKI AREA

A description of the ski area from 1978 included 3 rope tows, 4 ski slopes and lights for night skiing. Arrowhead also offered rentals and had a ski school. There was even a small lodge with a few vending machines and a snack bar. A very active racing program was also held at the resort each winter.

Main ski slope at Arrowhead
Author's collection

This ski area was a favorite of the Central Jersey Ski Club. They held many different events on the slopes. During the summer seasons of the early 1980s they even tried out the new short lived sport of grass skiing.

Ski slope and rope tow shack
Author's collection

ARROWHEAD SKI AREA

This little ski area also had a staff of several National Ski Patrol members. The West Slope at the Arrowhead ski area was dedicated and opened during the winter of 1978. Lift tickets were $3 on week days and $4 on weekends. The YMCA Camp Arrowhead is still open, but skiing seems to have ended here in 1985. The hills are still used today, but only for sleigh riding.

SKI LESSONS FOR NEW SKIERS

ARROWHEAD SKI AREA, MARLBORO

Our qualified ski instructors will introduce you to a sport you never knew could be so easy. C'mon out and learn to ski!

EARLY BIRD LESSONS
YOUTH & ADULTS

OCTOBER 23 thru NOVEMBER 4
3 lesson series on ski mats
$12.75 plus $10 YMCA Membership
Rentals Available
CALL 946-4598 TO SIGN UP NOW!

Early season lesson brochure
Courtesy of Camp Arrowhead

ARROWHEAD SKI AREA

Author's collection

Old lodge at YMCA Camp Arrowhead
Author's Collection

CHAPTER 9

BELLE MOUNTAIN
15 Valley Road
Hopewell Township

Ski area brochure courtesy of Mercer County Park System

View of the warming hut and rental shack
Author's collection

The Belle Mountain ski area opened in 1960. There were 5 trails with 1 chair lift and 1 rope tow. The ski area only had rope tows until 1971 when the chair lift was installed. The vertical drop of the longest run was 190 feet.

When I visited this ski area I came across some local residents who told me that Belle Mountain was affectionately known as Belle Bump. It was run for many years by the Mercer County Park System.

Belle Mountain was on the border of New Jersey – just across from New Hope, Pennsylvania. It had a small warming hut with a snack bar at the base, as well as a small trailer that was set up as a rental shop. As small as this mountain was, it had 4 ski instructors at the ski area.

Newspaper articles I found said that in 1993 Mercer County residents could ski here for only $16 during the week and only $21 on the weekends. Belle Mountain also offered something unique – a whole family could all get lift tickets during the week for only one fee of $20.

BELLE MOUNTAIN

Unfortunately Belle Mountain was another ski area that experienced some financial problems and several warm winters over the years. There were even a few years that it didn't open at all.

The ski area temporarily closed down in 1998 to look at its financial picture. Unfortunately it never reopened and New Jersey lost another one of the great little ski areas in the state.

Ski slope at Belle Mountain
Author's collection

There are plans to keep the old ski area property as open space and possibly turn it into some kind of nature park.

Another view of one of the slopes at Belle Mountain - Author's collection

CHAPTER 10

BERTHIAUME'S HIGH POINT SKI WAYS
Route 23
Montague

Rope tow base at Berthiaume's - Author's collection

Rodolphe Berthiaume was the owner of the property where this small ski hill was built. It was located on the left side of Route 23 in Montague near Fidler's Elbow as you are heading down the mountain towards Port Jervis, New York.

A local resident remembered a small food store also being located near the ski hill. It was reported that in the early days of New Jersey's ski history this small store was the last place to buy food before heading up the mountain from Port Jervis, NY to the High Point State Park.

BERTHIAUME'S HIGH POINT SKI WAYS

By today's standards Berthiaume's was an extremely small ski hill. It did have a ski lodge and two rope tows. One area resident said the slopes were very short and that people used very short skis there. One Montague resident said that some of the first Ski Doos were also used here. The slopes ran down a hillside starting from Route 23 to the shore of Lake Diane. Besides skiing, there was also ice skating on the lake. In the off season there was also skeet shooting over the other side of the lake. Berthiaume's was also known as the High Point Ski Ways.

Some local residents who remembered the ski hill said that Roy Rogers, the famous actor, was known to ski here. He also skied at some of the other small ski hills in the local area.

When Roy Rogers skied here, everyone that worked at the ski hill were not allowed let anyone else know that he was there.

It was also reported that Roy kept his famous horse, Trigger, at one of the local farms nearby.

Ski slope at Berthiaume's High Point Ski Ways – Author's collection

This ski hill only operated for a short time during the 1960s. It is possible that this small ski area may have been another one that was forced out of business by the opening of the Great Gorge South ski area in Vernon in the 1960s.

CHAPTER 11

CAMP MIDVALE
Snake Den Road
Ringwood

Camp Midvale ski hill - Author's collection

Camp Midvale was built in the 1920s by an organization that was called The Nature Friends of America. The recreation camp quickly became a popular weekend retreat for many of the local German, Polish and Russian immigrants.

There was a brick lodge with a dormitory, some small rental cabins, a stream fed swimming pool and several recreation fields at the camp. In the 1930s visitors stayed in the cabins or in the lodge for only $0.25 a night. Many daily recreation activities were offered such as volleyball, soccer, baseball, basketball, hiking and swimming.

Many residents from Ringwood and the surrounding area also frequented Camp Midvale. Some of them that I spoke to had very fond memories of the place.

CAMP MIDVALE

> **FOR THAT HOLIDAY SPIRIT**
> **CAMP MIDVALE**
> PRESENTS
> *Merry Christmas*
> &
> *Happy New Year*
> **WEEKENDS**
> All Complete — Excluding Sleeping Arrangements
> All meals (and what meals!) — Entertainment — Holiday Festivities
> Ice Skating Galore and Winter Sports
> From Sat. Night to Sunday Noon — Dec. 24th & 25th — Dec. 31st & Jan. 1st
> $1.20 Per Day for Members and Non-Members
> Make all arrangements at least one week in advance. — Write to **NF CAMP COMMITTEE, c/o Nature Friends, Midvale, N. J. or 11 W. 18th St., N. Y. C.** or your Respective Locals
> COME ONE   COME ALL

Advertisement from 1935 issue of Nature Friends Newsletter

The Erie Railroad ran through Haskell, Wanaque and Midvale, and continued through Ringwood. Visitors that were going to the camp were dropped off at the Midvale train station and then driven over to the resort.

Skiing at Camp Midvale started in the 1930s. A local resident told me that there was a rope tow on this slope. It was operated by an engine from an old 1930s Ford Model A car that was at the top of the hill on cinder blocks.

The ski hill was located on a small slope next to a stream fed swimming pool. When this hill was first used for skiing, people didn't really know how to make any turns with their long wooden skis, so they just headed straight down the slope. Some of the skiers also held contests to see who could make it the furthest across the recreation field before stopping.

Skiing ended here in the early 1970s. May and Walter Weis bought the property in 1974 and shortly after that this area became known as the Weis Ecology Center. The Weis family operated the old camp as an educational nature park that was always open to the public for free.

CAMP MIDVALE

The National Audubon Society took over the property in 1995 and it is still operated as an educational nature park. The Weis Ecology Center offers cross-country skiing as well as lessons in the winter when there is enough snow.

One of the cabins at Camp Midvale – Author's collection

Most of the wide open slope has now grown over. There is one hiking trail that still runs up the hillside. If you look carefully you can find one of the rope tow pulleys on a tree where the rope tow was operated.

Beverly E. Allen - started Camp Midvale

Old rope tow pulley - Author's collection

63

CAMP MIDVALE

Old rope tow pulley – Author's collection

Remains of ski slope – Author's collection

CHAPTER 12

CAMPGAW MOUNTAIN
Campgaw Road
Mahwah

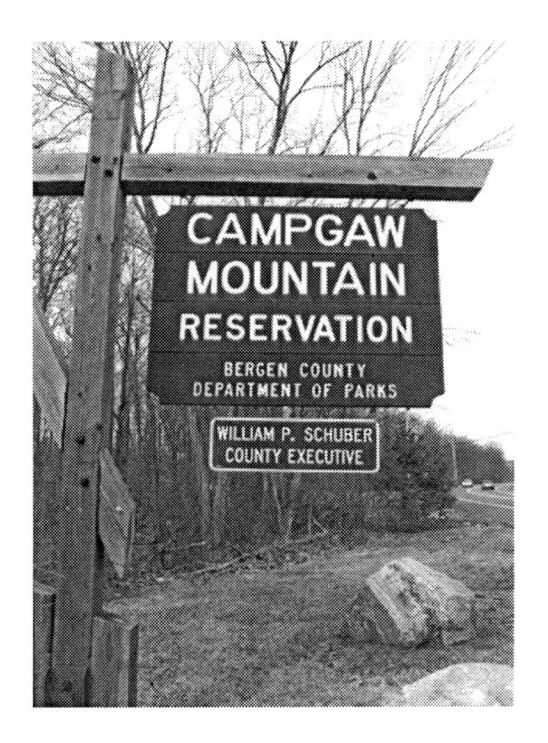

Campgaw Mountain has a very interesting history. The Army Corps of Engineers built a Nike Missile Base there in 1955. The missile base was run by the Army's 483rd Anti-Aircraft Guided Missile Battalion.

The base was known as the Nike Missile Battery NY 93/94. Descriptions of it said the control area was at the top of the mountain and that there was a military housing development near the launch site.

The Campgaw Mountain ski area opened in 1961. The missile site was still in operation during that time.

Entrance sign for Campgaw Mountain Reservation - Author's collection

Management at the Campgaw Mountain ski area changed several times over the years. It is now being run by the Bergen County Parks Association.

The missile base began closing down in 1968. It was finally dismantled in 1971. Some of the old buildings are still on the property, but have been converted for the park and ski area's use.

Facilities at the ski area include a small lodge with a ski shop, rental area and a snack bar. There are also two double chair lifts, 2 rope tows and a T-Bar. The mountain has 8 trails and they all have lights for night skiing. The vertical drop of the highest slope is 270 feet. Believe it or not you can still find two old Hall double chair lifts there that are still running.

CAMPGAW MOUNTAIN

Campgaw Mountain is one of the few ski areas in New Jersey that is still open. It's a small but really friendly place to ski if you don't want to travel far and don't like big crowds.

Lodge and rental shop - Author's collection

One of the trails at Campgaw Mountain – Author's collection

CHAPTER 13

CRAIGMEUR SKI AREA
Green Pond Road
Newfoundland

Entrance sign to Craigmeur Ski Area - Author's collection

Craigmeur's status in New Jersey's ski history is extremely important. It was the first official ski area in the state in 1937. It was also the longest continually operating ski area and the largest "learn to ski area" in New Jersey.

Craigmeur was called a reverse ski area. The parking lot and the lodge were at the top of the slopes.

Hugo Meury and several other Swiss immigrants opened the ski area on property that Hugo bought on the Copperas Mountain range in 1937. The ski area originally started with just one small slope and a rope tow for Hugo's family and friends. Some old newspaper reports said that Hugo named the ski area after his wife – Helen Craig and himself, hence the name "Craigmeur". After she died, he expanded the ski area and opened it to the public.

CRAIGMEUR SKI AREA

Original lodge and rope tow - Courtesy of Ray Schank - Craigmeur

There were a lot of firsts at Craigmeur. The rope tow at this ski area was said to be the first one in New Jersey. It also had some of the first snow making equipment in the state in 1955.

From 1963 to 1967 the ski area also had a ski jump. Art Tokle, Sr. from the Odin Ski Club in Lake Telemark was one of the designers of the jump. The original ski jump was only about 30 meters long. Some of the old newspaper articles described one of the ski jumps as having 3 different start areas on it. The runway was described as being 128 feet long with an angle of 30 degrees.

Unfortunately the ski jumps here had some bad luck. The first ski jump was destroyed by strong winds. The second one was built immediately after the first one and several competitions were held on it before it burned down in a fire that also destroyed the original ski lodge.

CRAIGMEUR SKI AREA

Old newspaper photo of Art Tokle, Sr. at the top of the Craigmeur ski jump
Courtesy of Ray Schank - Craigmeur

Arnie Kirbach, Sr. was a ski instructor at Craigmeur for a few seasons. When I talked with him he told me that if Hugo Meury saw you fall on the slopes and you bunched up the snow in one spot or made a hole (better known as a Sitzmark) and you didn't smooth out the snow, he would ask you to leave. Hugo's thinking was that if people also kept skiing in the same area of the slopes they would ruin the runs for the other people. Craigmeur also had no snow making at this point.

A beginner skier on the slopes
Courtesy of Ray Schank - Craigmeur

CRAIGMEUR SKI AREA

During the winter of 1942, Hugo ran some white Christmas lights down the side of one of the slopes. These were probably some of the first electric lights used for night skiing.

In the 1950s some of the trips up to the ski area were pretty amazing. Many skiers would drive up the mountain and not see snow anywhere, but when they arrived at Craigmeur, the ski slopes would be covered with snow. Hugo Meury's secret was that he removed all of the dead grass and other vegetation from the slopes before the winter. He also took time to grow a lot of moss on the slopes. Arnie Kirbach, Sr. believed that was what made the snow last longer.

Artist's rendering of Craigmeur (includes the old ski jump – also shows a proposed hotel that was never built.) Courtesy of Ray Schank - Craigmeur

This little ski area is probably the first place where many people in New Jersey learned how to ski. At one time they had 65 ski instructors.
They offered something unique for ski lessons. A skier could purchase a coupon booklet for 5 ski lessons. You could take your 5 ski lessons any time you wanted to. You could even take them all in one day if you wanted to.

The slopes at Craigmeur only had a 270 foot vertical, but for a first time skier, the slopes looked like they had a 1,000 foot vertical or more. Once you got your courage up, you told yourself that if you could ski the "steep" slopes here, you could ski anything!

CRAIGMEUR SKI AREA

In 1961 the Craigmeur Ski Club formed and several weekly meetings were held at the ski area. It was unique during this time period for a ski club to hold its business meetings at a ski area. Several years later the location of the Craigmeur Ski Club's meetings changed.

The owners of Craigmeur changed several times. Hugo Meury was the original owner. Stan Udel was another one of the owners. Dorothy Murray and her husband took over the ski area in 1965. She was still the owner of the Craigmeur ski area when it closed down in 1998. She is the longest continual owner of a ski area in New Jersey.

Main slope and t-bar at Craigmeur
Courtesy of Ray Schank - Craigmeur

During one of the expansions some new offices, a rental shop and a new cafeteria were added to the resort. New slopes were also added. The length of the trails were also extended to 1,700 feet.

Descriptions of the Craigmeur ski area included a learner's area, 3 open slopes, 2 trails, a double chair lift, a T-Bar, 2 rope tows and a ski school.

In 1970 lift tickets at Craigmeur were about $4 on week days and $6 on weekends. In 1978 a summer picnic area and recreation area was added to the ski area.

When the ski area closed down in 1998, they sold off most of their equipment to other local ski areas. Here's something unbelievable too! I was told that one of the snow cats from Craigmeur is now being used in Hawaii on Mauna Kea Mountain. Mauna Kea is 14,000 feet high and the only way to get up the mountain is to walk up, use a 4-wheel drive vehicle, or by using the snow cat. You can ski on Mauna Kea, but there are no lifts and there is no ski lodge. It almost sounds a little like Tuckerman's Ravine. The snow cat is used to get researchers up to the 12 observatories that are located on the mountain. When there is extra room, skiers are also taken up.

CRAIGMEUR SKI AREA

People skied at Craigmeur for over 60 years before they closed the ski trails.

Their summer picnic business was run from 1978 to 2005. Dorothy Murray sold the 67 acre Craigmeur property to the Morris County Parks Commission in summer of 2005. The property is now preserved as open space.

Craigmeur ski lodge & ski jump
Courtesy of Ray Schank - Craigmeur

Author's collection

CHAPTER 14

GALLOPING HILL SKI AREA
Galloping Hill Golf Course
Kenilworth

Picture from New Jersey Ski Areas © 1968 by NJ Dept. Conservation & Economic Development

GALLOPING HILL SKI AREA

The Galloping Hill golf course opened in Kenilworth in 1926. During the 1940s and early 1950s some of the golf course property was sold off for the development of the Garden State Parkway.

This little ski center opened in the 1940s on the 3rd fairway of the 9 hole golf course. The vertical drop of the main slope was only 100 feet. It was a wide open slope that was 800 feet long. A rope tow that was 675 feet long serviced the main slope.

There were also two metal toboggan chutes on the 10th fairway of the golf course.

Galloping Hill's ski slope was only open when there was enough natural snow. In 1970 six snow making guns were added to the slope. This allowed the slope to be open longer through the winter season. There were also lights on the slope for night skiing. Skiing ended here in the 1980s.

The Galloping Hill Golf Course also had a sleigh riding hill that people used to refer to as "Suicide Hill".

CHAPTER 15

GREAT GORGE SKI AREAS
Route 94
McAfee

Ski patch - Author's collection

GREAT GORGE SOUTH

Before they built the Great Gorge ski area in 1965, Jack Kurlander and John Fitzgerald worked for a lumber company. The Baker family was also heavily involved in the development of this ski area. While working at the Snow Bowl ski area in Milton, they sold bonds for $1,000 each to help cover the costs of the construction and purchasing the land. The new ski area was built on Hamburg Mountain on property that was known as the Frederick's farm.

The ski area opened with just a few slopes and several ski lifts. The resort later expanded to the South peak with more trails and chair lifts. The ski lifts at Great Gorge were all made by the Borvig Lift Company of Pine Island, New York. They were installed by the Dolomite Ski Construction Company which was also located in Pine Island.

GREAT GORGE SKI AREAS

GREAT GORGE SOUTH

The original lodge at Great Gorge South was designed by Sandy McIlvane. It had 2 restaurants, 2 cafeterias, and 2 different bars. The Great Gorge South resort also had a small mid-mountain warming hut that sold some snacks and drinks. Another small lodge was located at the top of the slopes. Most of the original furniture in the Great Gorge South's base lodge came from one of the exhibits from the 1964/1965 World's Fair that which was held in Flushing Meadow, New York.

Otto Schniebs and Luis Schlafflinger designed the ski runs at Great Gorge. The vertical drop of the mountain was 1,040 feet. The ski area had 24 trails. 8 chairs and 2 rope tows carried skiers up the slopes.

What originally made Great Gorge South extremely popular was that it was much bigger than the Craigmeur ski area in nearby Newfoundland, and that it was only 1 hour from New York City. Vernon's new ski area provided daily and weekend skiing for anyone that did not want to travel to New York State, Pennsylvania or Vermont.

Great Gorge South grew to also include its own dedicated ski racing trail where many young skiers got their start in racing. Jack Kurlander's daughter, Jamie, also spent many hours on the racing trail here. She went on to become a member of the U.S. Ski Team.

Picture of Great Gorge South slopes - Author's collection

GREAT GORGE SKI AREAS

GREAT GORGE SOUTH

In 1968 there was a 30 meter ski jump built at this resort. It was used for many local competitions over the years. Art Tokle, Jr. said that in 1968 plastic sheets were put down on the jump hill so they could hold an early season jump competition. You can still see some old remains of the ski jump on a hill just above the beginner learning area at what is now known as the Mountain Creek South ski area.

In 1970 the Great Gorge resort was the first ski area in the world to use a jet engine to power their snow making equipment. The owners of the ski area worked with several people from the Curtiss-Wright Company to develop the new snow making system. A J-65 jet engine was converted and they were able to cover the slopes with artificial snow much faster than any of the other ski areas.

The Head Ski Company introduced their new fiberglass skis at the Great Gorge South ski area in February 1971.

During the summer season the ski area was also open for various events. Scenic rides were given on the chairlifts, outdoor concerts and small festivals were held there.

On June 1, 1970 a small zoo was also built near the beginner ski slope. It was open until October 15th each year. The zoo was another idea to bring in money during the off season.

The zoo was opened by Bob Dietch, who worked for the Ringling Brother's Circus. It was set up at the end of the base lodge and went back to the beginner ski slope area. A small kiddie playland and a refreshment area were also included.

Old brochure from Great Gorge South & North
Author's collection

GREAT GORGE SKI AREAS

GREAT GORGE SOUTH

In the winter, the animals were kept at a local farm near the Waywayanda State Park on Warwick Turnpike. Remnants of some of the animal cages can still be found on the beginner slope.

For a limited time the Susquehanna and New Jersey Transit ran special ski trains out to the Great Gorge South ski area during the 1970s and 1980s. It was really convenient for skiers because the ski trains stopped right at the resort's parking lot, which was across the street from the ski slopes.

The Great Gorge South ski area was open for 33 years before it closed in 1997.

Old news photo of Great Gorge South ski lodge

GREAT GORGE NORTH

Jack Kurlander built this ski area on Hamburg Mountain in 1971. A connecting trail was also put in to link it up with the Great Gorge South ski area just down the road.

There was only a small warming hut at the base of the trails when it first opened. Original plans for this ski resort included a large Olympic ski jump area, it was never built. When the Playboy Club Hotel was built across the road in 1971, a cable car was going to be installed that would have carried skiers directly from the hotel to the slopes. Unfortunately it was also never built.

GREAT GORGE SKI AREAS

GREAT GORGE SOUTH

The Great Gorge North resort included 14 trails with a vertical drop of 980 feet. It opened with only one chair lift servicing the slopes. There were also lights for night skiing and snow making equipment here.

This new ski resort was connected to the already established Great Gorge South resort by a trail that traversed the middle of the mountain as well as a chair lift.

In 1986 the new village at Great Gorge South was built that included the Kites restaurant, a health spa, a small hotel and a condominium complex.

GREAT GORGE NORTH

Warm winters during the 1970s and some financial difficulties due to the rising insurance premiums it had to carry. In 1971 the Great Gorge ski areas were forced to close down. In the early 1970s both of the ski areas were merged with the Vernon Valley ski resort. In 1974 the Vernon Valley/Great Gorge resort was purchased by the Great American Recreation Company. The resorts filed for bankruptcy in 1995.

The resorts were not able to operate in 1996 and in 1997 they shut down their operations for what looked to be the last time. In 1998 the ski areas were purchased by Intrawest and were able to reopen for the 1998/1999 ski season.

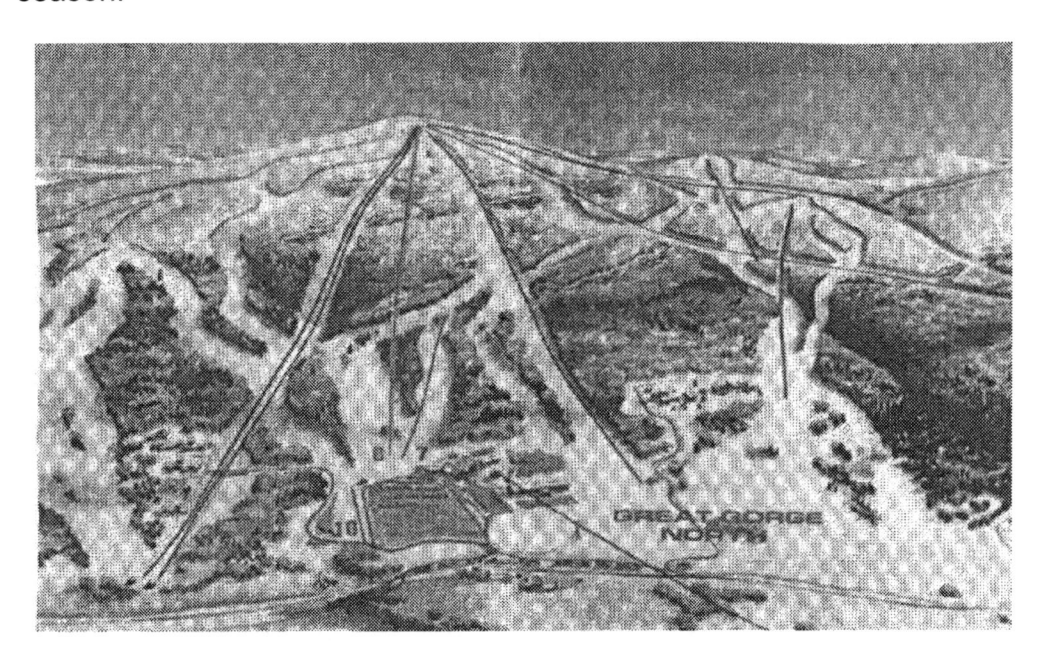

Map of Great Gorge North ski area

GREAT GORGE SKI AREAS

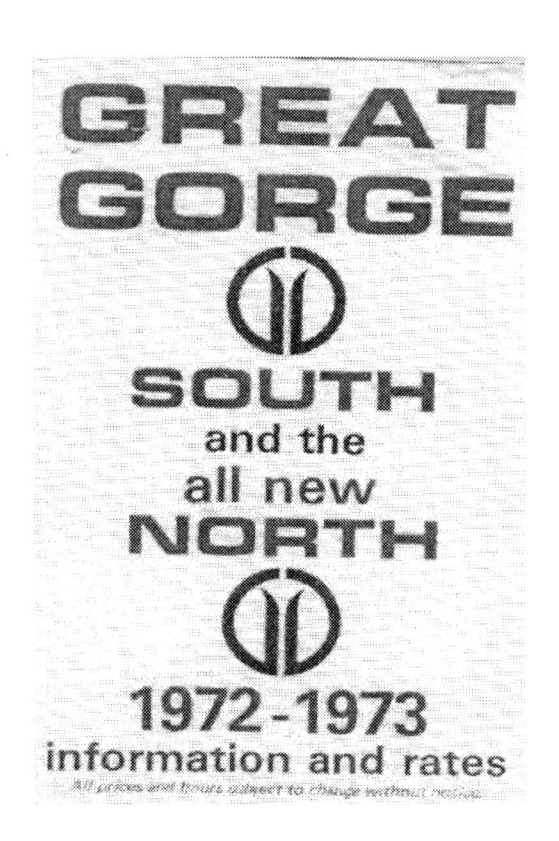

Old brochure from Great Gorge South & North

Great Gorge ski pin – Author's collection

Listing of trails at Great Gorge South & Great Gorge North

CHAPTER 16

HIDDEN VALLEY
Breakneck Road
Vernon

Plans for this Vernon ski area were started in the summer of 1975. Newspaper reports said that Jack Kurlander was one of the people who built this ski area.

Breakneck Road was usually closed during the winter seasons before the Hidden Valley ski area was built. The town felt that it was too dangerous for people to drive down in the snow. Anyone that has driven on Breakneck Road can probably guess how the road might have gotten its name.

Ski patch from Author's collection

The Hidden Valley ski area opened in 1976. When it first opened, it was operated as a private ski club. The general public was originally only permitted to ski there on week nights and weekend nights. Several years later it was totally opened to the public. Hidden Valley was the first ski area in the state to allow snow boarders on its slopes.

The ski lodge here is a beautiful 3 level A-frame structure. There are large windows and several decks that look out over the slopes. All of the chairs and tables that were originally in the cafeteria and the old bar stools were bought from the Snow Bowl ski area when it closed. The double chair lift that stands on the Chicken Delight slope was also bought from the Snow Bowl ski area. Some equipment that was used at Hidden Valley was also bought from the Holly Mountain ski area in Lower Alloways Creek when it closed.

The Hidden Valley ski area has 12 trails and 3 chair lifts. The vertical drop of the slopes is 620 feet. There is also snow making equipment. Lights are on the mountain so it is also open in the evenings.

HIDDEN VALLEY

The New Jersey Ski Racing Association operates out of the ski area. Hidden Valley has a very active ski and snow board racing program for children and adults. This mountain has the only F.I.S. sanctioned racing trail in New Jersey.

This is a four season resort that also provides activities such as a swimming pool, tennis courts, volleyball, baseball and a picnic area located at the top of the slopes.

The ski slopes of Hidden Valley are surrounded by some beautiful town houses. In the off season Hidden Valley plays host to many weddings, parties and outdoor activities. There is also a restaurant at the resort that is open all year long.

Hidden Valley is one of the few ski areas in New Jersey that is still open.

Main chair lift and a trail at Hidden Valley
Author's collection

Main lodge at Hidden Valley – Author's collection

Entrance sign – Author's collection

CHAPTER 17

HIGH POINT SKI CENTER
High Point State Park
High Point

Skiers at High Point State Park © 1930s - Courtesy of High Point State Park

Col. Anthony Kuser and his wife loved this area so much that they donated over 10,000 acres of land to the state of New Jersey in April 1923 to create New Jersey's first state park. The park sits on top of the highest point in the state at 1,803 feet. Several newspapers reported that the High Point State Park opened on May 23, 1923. The park is still open and is visited by thousands of people every year.

The original High Point Inn was built in 1890. When the Kuser family owned the mansion, it was also used as a hunting lodge for Col. Anthony Kuser. Unfortunately the High Point Inn fell into major disrepair over the years and was demolished in 1996.

President Franklin Delano Roosevelt's tree army - the Civilian Conservation Corps had several camps at the park from around 1933 to 1942. The men from camps 216 & 1289 were responsible for clearing most of the hiking trails and constructing most of the buildings in the park. They also built the tall memorial monument and also cleared the slopes that were used for skiing.

HIGH POINT SKI CENTER

Ads in the newspapers for High Point called it "Little Switzerland." The new winter sports center officially opened on December 28, 1936. There were also miles of trails for cross-country skiing, two lakes for ice skating, a ski jump and several open slopes for skiing. The slope of the ski jump had a 350 vertical drop. There are reports that the Swedish Ski Club as well as several other local ski clubs held many winter sports competitions in the park.

Early skiers at High Point State Park © 1930s - Courtesy High Point State Park

In the late 1930s and early 1940s the L. Bamberger Company sponsored Erie railroad snow trains that ran from Newark and several other parts of New Jersey to the train station in Port Jervis, New York. Skiers and skaters were then picked up by a special bus and taken up to the park. The High Point Inn also had overnight opportunities for any guests that wanted to spend a few days at the park.

There were two different ski hills in the park. The first was High Point Ski Center which ran down a hillside near Lake Marcia. A 350 foot long ski jump was also located there.

The second ski slopes ran down the hillside near Steeneykill Lake. Some skiers even used the road that leads up to the War Memorial Tower as a ski run.

HIGH POINT SKI CENTER

Travelers arrive from Port Jervis, NY train station © 1930s - Courtesy of High Point State Park

Had there been snow making equipment on the alpine slopes, this small ski hill may have operated longer than it did. Downhill skiing operated here on and off for many years. It seems that it finally ended in the 1960s just before the opening of the Great Gorge ski area in McAfee.

The High Point State Park still has an extremely active cross-country skiing program that has its own small lodge and several miles of ski trails. There is also snow making equipment and grooming equipment on the cross-country trails.

HIGH POINT SKI CENTER

Remains of High Point Ski Center ski jump run.
Courtesy of the Friends of High Point State Park

Opening day of the High Point Ski Center.
Picture from Newark Evening News © 1936

High Point Ski Center patch
Courtesy of John Keator – Superintendent of High Point State Park

CHAPTER 18
HOLIDAY LAKE SKI CENTER
Clove Road
Montague

Before it became an exclusive lake community, this area was originally farmland.

The property was originally owned by the local Grathwohl, Wainright, Westbrook and DeGroat families. This new lake development was first known as Canyon Ridge. It later became known as Holiday Lake.

The private resort community of the Holiday Lake Country Club was built in 1966 in Montague. The 1,000 acre private club was originally advertised as both a summer and winter recreation area.

Old Holiday Lake ads show that it offered many different sporting opportunities such as tennis, volleyball, swimming, fishing, golfing and skiing.

1st ski hill near the pipeline - Author's collection

Picture from New Jersey Ski Areas – NJ Dept. Conservation © 1968

HOLIDAY LAKE SKI CENTER

There were two ski hills at Holiday Lake. Gib Roby built his first rope tow on the pipeline that is located on the club's property. The trail was 1,500 feet long with a 210 foot vertical drop. The trail was about 100 feet wide. It had 1 rope tow. There were lights on the slope for night skiing.

The second rope tow that Gib Roby built on the club's property was on the 7th hole to the 9th hole of the golf course. There were no lights on this slope.

There are still remnants of the old rope tow pulleys on the side of the golf course.

2nd ski hill at Holiday Lake - Author's collection

There was no charge for lift tickets here because the slopes were only open to the members of the Holiday Lake Country Club. Skiing was available every day.

2nd ski hill on golf course - Author's collection

HOLIDAY LAKE SKI CENTER

Unfortunately skiing ended here in the 1970s. The Holiday Lake Country Club became what is known today as the Highpoint Country Club and it is open to the public.

Rope tow pulley remains on golf course
Author's collection

Sign from Highpoint Country Club
Picture from Author's collection

HOLIDAY LAKE SKI CENTER

panoramic HOLIDAY LAKE

Spring and Brook-fed, over 2 miles long. A sloping naturally wooded shoreline and acres of sandy beaches, perfect for swimming and boating, surrounded by . . .

A Picturesque Golf Course already completed and playable, playing back and forth across the lake. Then consider . . .

Hunting on our private New Jersey club premises as well as our other lands in New York and Pennsylvania, all offering the finest in deer and small game hunting, or . . .

Fishing for rainbow, brown and brook trout in our well-stocked lake with its trout hatchery, and accompanying fast running private stream, or trying for pike, bass and shad in the Delaware River, one mile away, or . . .

Sledding, ice skating and beginners skiing at the excellent facilities provided by us, or . . .

Horseback riding, hiking, picnicking and all the field sports playable on our athletic fields with four baseball diamonds and track, or participate in any one of the dozens of other sporting or recreational activities too numerous to mention but available for your enjoyment and to further one's physical fitness.

Please accept this message as a sincere invitation to you and to your family to visit Holiday Lake, to go through all of our many completely different furnished models, and to actually see for yourselves the outstanding recreational community which this brochure attempts to depict.

Courtesy of Montague Association for the Restoration of Community History (M.A.R.C.H.)

CHAPTER 19

HOLLY MOUNTAIN SKI AREA
Hell Neck Road
Lower Alloways Creek

Holly Mountain brochure

Holly Mountain opened in the early 1970s. This ski area was located the furthest south in New Jersey. Rich and Florence Wood were the original owners before the town of Lower Alloways Creek bought it from them in 1978. Believe it or not this ski area did not sell any alcoholic beverages. There was a huge sign posted at the beginning of the driveway to this ski hill stating that.

HOLLY MOUNTAIN

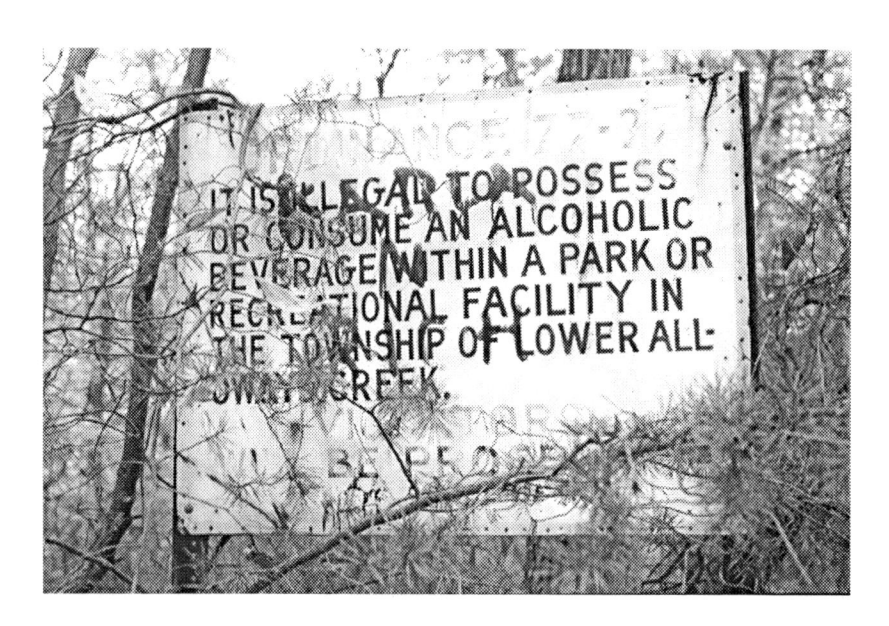

No alcohol sign at entrance of Holly Mountain - Author's collection

Holly Mountain had 3 small slopes with 6 trails. The vertical drop was 150 feet. One of the steepest runs was called Kamakazee Hill. This small ski area did have a lodge. The mountain also had lights for night skiing. Since it was in the southern part of New Jersey there was also snow making at this ski area. The slopes and trails were serviced by one chair lift and one rope tow. It was a reverse ski area because the lodge and the parking lot were at the top of the slopes instead of at the bottom. Holly Mountain was a very small ski hill and it could not really compete with the larger ski areas just over the Pennsylvania border in the Poconos.

Picture of Holly Mountain lodge - from '88/'89 Holly Mountain brochure

HOLLY MOUNTAIN

This little ski area had a 3 level lodge. There were 3 full time ski instructors who taught the American Teknik and the Graduated Length Method. In 1979 lift tickets for adults were only $8.00 during weekdays, and $9.00 on the weekends and holidays. Daily rental equipment cost between $7.75 and $8.75.

This ski area closed in 1986 mostly because the winters weren't staying cold enough to keep the snow on the slopes. When Holly Mountain closed, all of the lift equipment was sold off. There is nothing left of this old ski area now except for a few snow making pipes and the cement bases of the chair lifts.

Chair lift base - Author's collection

Ski slope at Holly Mountain - Author's collection

HOLLY MOUNTAIN

LODGE
PONY LIFT   PARKING

CHAIR LIFT

LEGEND

① Beginners   ② Intermediate

③ Advanced Intermediate

- △ A Dog House Run
- △ B Green Berry Slope
- △ C Red Berry Run
- △ D Snow Bird
- △ E Kamakazi
- △ F Hells Neck Run

At Holly Mountain we strongly believe in the alpine tradition, hospitality, so we've built a three story lodge for you at the summit of our mountain. A lodge that offers the comforts and refreshments that make it an enjoyable day or night of skiing, with it's snack bar and lounging room for relaxing and enjoying the view from it's balcony. We offer a double chair lift to our intermediate, advanced intermediate skiers and a pony lift for our beginners.

HOLLY MOUNTAIN SKI AREA is a member

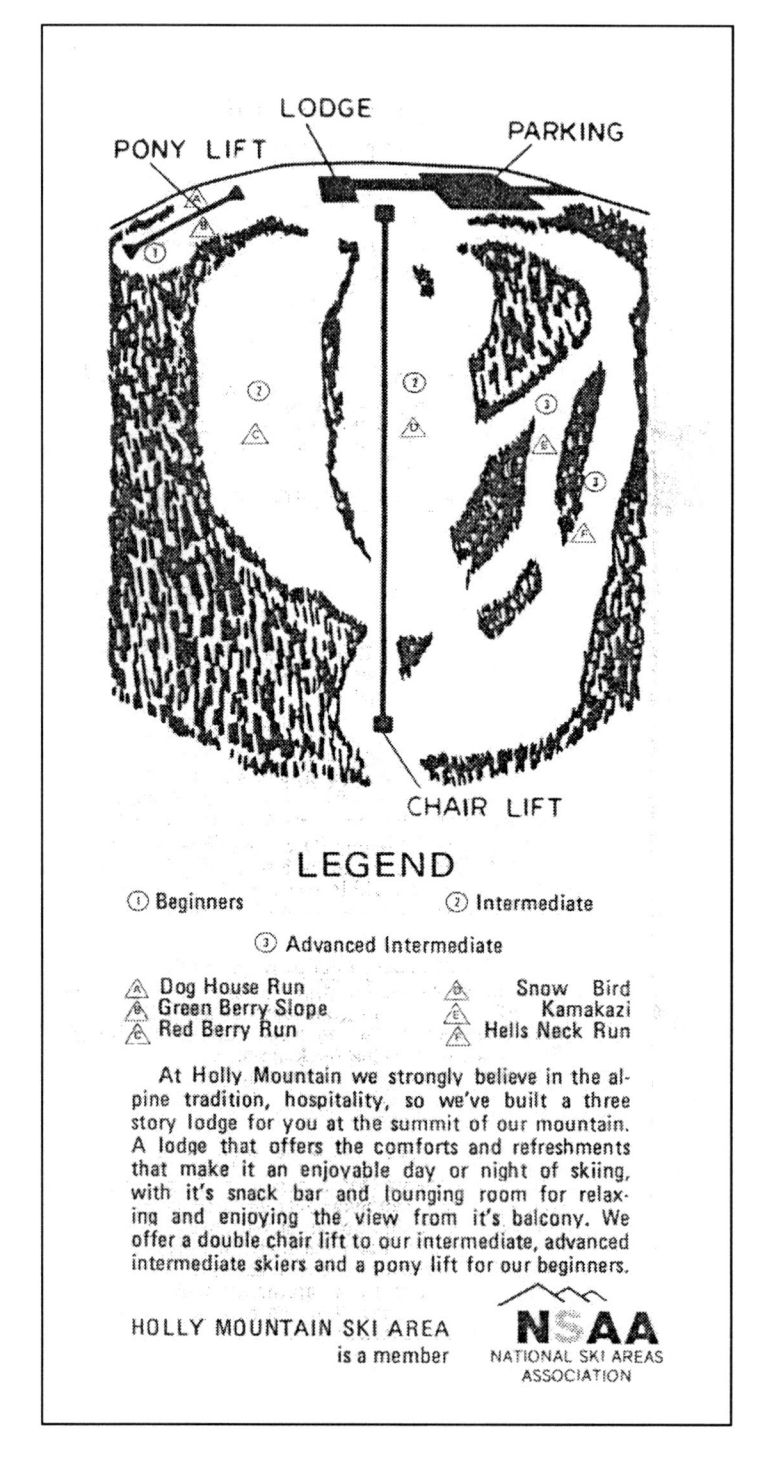

NSAA — NATIONAL SKI AREAS ASSOCIATION

Slope layout – from Holly Mountain brochure

CHAPTER 20

HOLMDEL SKI AREA
Longstreet Road
Holmdel Township

Ski slope at Holmdel ski area - Author's collection

There was a listing for this ski area in a booklet that was published in 1964 by the New Jersey Department of Conservation.

The slope opened for skiing in the 1960s. There was only 1 wide open slope here. The vertical drop was 240 feet. When people wanted to take another run, they had to walk back up, because there was no rope tow or chair lift. Unfortunately this slope did not have any snow making.

There were no prices for lift tickets or use of this slope because it was in a county park. People could ski here from 8AM to 10PM during the week and 8AM to 12PM on the weekends.

HOLMDEL SKI AREA

During the late 1960s and early 1970s, James Truncer of the Monmouth County Park Commission was in charge of the skiing operations here. I was told that skiing ended here in the 1970s. The hill is still used today for sleigh riding.

Picture of Holmdel ski hill from 1964 New Jersey Dept. of Conservation ski area listing

CHAPTER 21

IDLEBRAE INN
Route 206
Montague

The ski hill at the Idlebrae Inn opened during the early 1960s.

Besides building the two rope tows at the Holiday Lake Country Club, Gib Roby was also responsible for installing the rope tow at this ski hill. Fred Merusi, a local resident, remembered skiing here during the winters of 1963 and 1964. He told me that a 1954 Ford station wagon engine was set up at the top of the slope to power the rope tow. The rope tow pulleys were attached to tall poles on the side of the slope next to a long stretch of pine trees. Unfortunately there was no snow making here.

Many of the guests who stayed at the hotel used this small ski hill. The ski trail ran down the hillside from the hotel to the restaurant on Route 206. Unfortunately this ski hill was short lived. It was only open until 1966.

The Idlebrae Inn was sold and became known as the Rendezvous Inn. It was last known as the Blackthorn Inn and Motel.

Ski hill at the Idlebrae Inn – Author's collection

IDLEBRAE INN

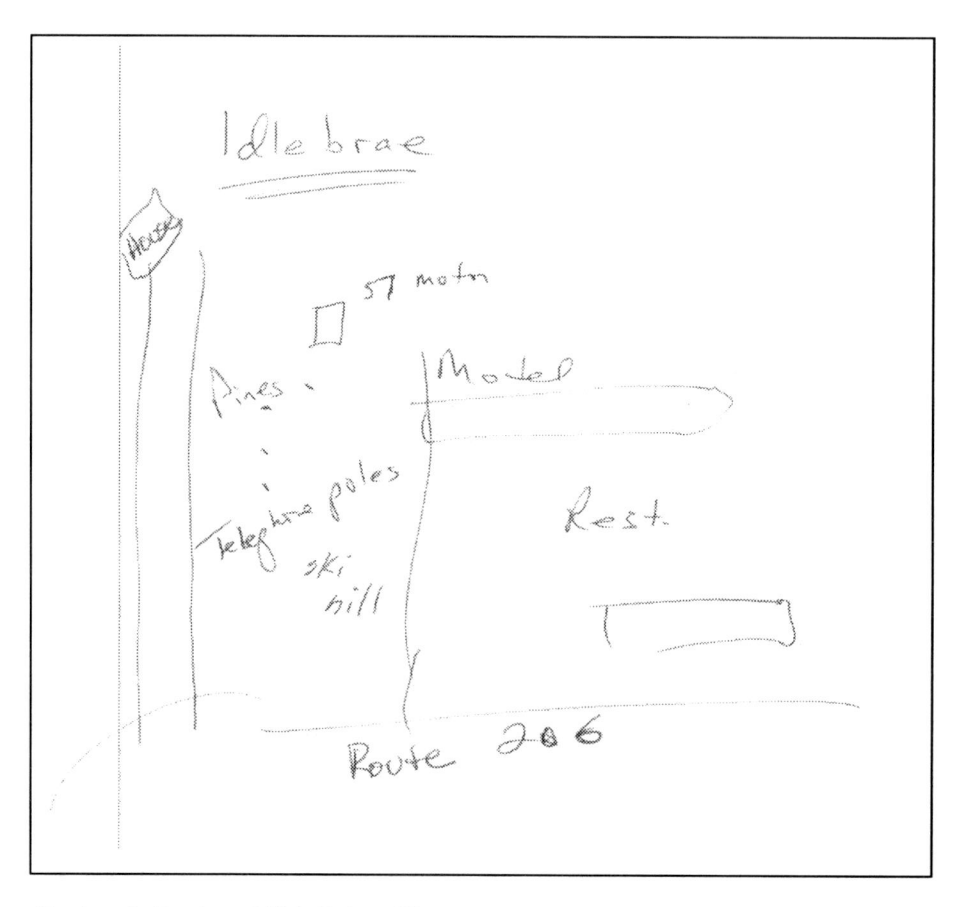

Map layout - Courtesy of Alicia Batko – (Montague Association for Restoration of Community History)

Former Idlebrae Restaurant - Author's collection

CHAPTER 22

JUGTOWN MOUNTAIN SKI AREA
Asbury

Jugtown Mountain's main slope and ski lodge - Courtesy of the Vones brothers

Frank Vones and his brothers Sam, Fred and Jim opened this ski area in 1961. When I spoke with Frank, he told me that he and his brothers all started in the construction industry. That helped them when they started building their new ski area.

The Jugtown Mountain ski area was located off of Route 78 West near Phillipsburg. The property for the Jugtown Mountain ski area was leased on a yearly basis from the Osmun family, who were the property owners.

JUGTOWN MOUNTAIN

Old newspaper reports said when the ski area opened it was bigger than the Craigmeur ski area that was in Newfoundland. Remember that when Craigmeur first opened in 1937, it only had one small slope and one short rope tow. Many of the additions to the Craigmeur ski area were not done until the late 1960s.

Frank Vones and his brothers started clearing the mountain in 1957 and built the ski lodge. The parking lot for was located in a field across the street. The main lodge was a one floor building with a fireplace, snack bar, rental shop. It also had lots of tables where people could eat their food or just relax. There are reports that Mrs. Osmun sold blue berry muffins every day at the ski area. Rumor has it that some people just came to Jugtown Mountain every day to get some of the fresh made muffins.

The Vones brothers all had experience in different areas of construction; they built their own snow making and grooming equipment for the ski area.

During my conversations with Frank and his brothers, they said they bought one of Jugtown Mountain's rope tows from the Mount Snow ski area in Vermont.

Several members of the Vones families and the Osmun family helped run the ski area.

Rope tow shack at top of main slope - Author's collection

Jugtown Mountain only had two ski slopes. There was one large 1,000 foot long slope. The vertical drop was 285 feet. A shack at the top of the slope housed the engine for one of the rope tows. The engine for the rope tow was taken from an old Ford Model A. A short distance up the main slope was another small rope tow that allowed skiers to only go part of the way up the main slope.

JUGTOWN MOUNTAIN

A smaller beginner's slope also ran along the side of the road that also had its own rope tow. Jugtown Mountain had 1 ski instructor.

The Lehigh Valley railroad ran through the area and one of the train stations was located right near the ski area. It was proposed that one of the stops would be at Jugtown Mountain so that skiers would be dropped off at the base of the Jugtown Mountain ski area. Unfortunately those plans never came to be.

Newspaper reports said in 1966 the lift ticket prices were about $4 and they were only about $5 in 1971.

A view from the top of Jugtown Mountain
Courtesy of the Vones family

Since the property was leased on a year to year basis, the Vones brothers hoped to make a deal with the property owners to further expand the ski area. Unfortunately the owners weren't interested in the ski area getting any larger. Jugtown Mountain closed down in 1971.

Frank "Bucky" Vones in the ticket booth - Courtesy of the Vones family

JUGTOWN MOUNTAIN

The Vones family at Jugtown Mountain © 1966 - Courtesy of the Vones family

Skiers at Jugtown Mountain - Courtesy of the Osmun family

CHAPTER 23

LAKE TELEMARK SKI JUMPS
Lake Telemark

Lake Telemark was known as Little Norway. The Lake Telemark development was started around 1925. The area is populated mostly by Norwegian families.

The Odin Ski Club started in 1948. Records from Lake Telemark show that Art Tokle, Sr. and Erling Flogland helped find the sites for the ski jumps.

The property where the first ski jump was built was originally owned by Sverre Justnes. Members of the Odin Ski Club helped clear the small hills and built the ski jumps. Art Tokle, Jr. and Ellen (Skavnes) Tonnesen told me that the ski jumps were in Lake Telemark from around 1948 to 1962.

There were two jumps at Lake Telemark. The junior jump was described as only being about 45 meters long. The second one was called Oslo Hill and was about 1,000 meters long. They were fairly short ski jumps compared to today's standards.

Lake Telemark ski jump - Courtesy of Ellen (Skavnes) Tonnesen

LAKE TELEMARK

The members of the Odin Ski Club participated in many of the ski jumping competitions held throughout the United States. The jumps at Lake Telemark were the site of the first sanctioned ski jumping competitions in New Jersey. Old newspaper reports said that one of the first jump contests was at the Lake Telemark's first annual Winter Carnival in 1948.

Ellen (Skavnes) Tonnesen told me that she was one of the first women ski jumpers on the East Coast in the late 1940s and early 1950s. When I talked with her, she told me that she participated in many of the Odin Ski Club's jump competitions in Lake Telemark. She also competed at the famous ski jump at Bear Mountain, New York. Her notoriety even got her a spot on the Ed Sullivan show in the early 1950s.

During June 1958 the Odin Ski Club held a jump competition held on crushed ice.

Ellen told me that her father developed the machine that made the crushed ice used on the jumps for their summer and fall competitions.

In reading some of the old newspaper reports it seems that some of the best ski jumpers in the United States also came to compete on the Lake Telemark ski jumps.

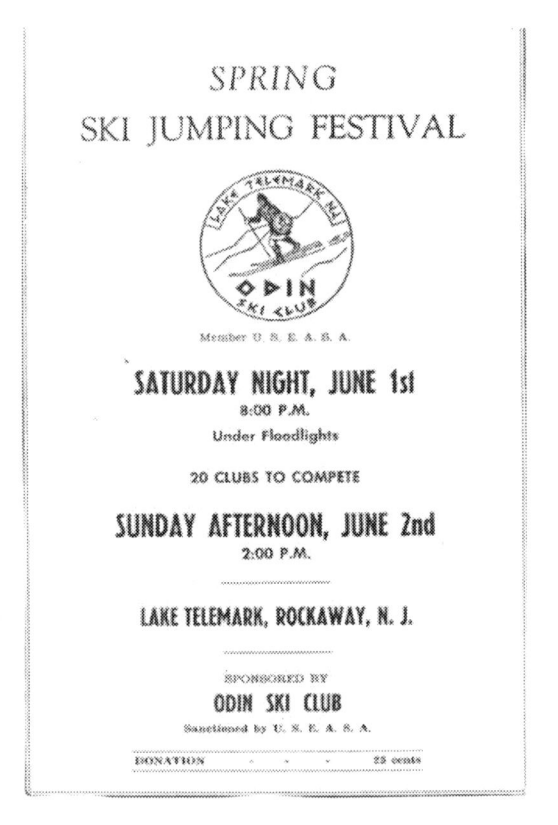

SPRING
SKI JUMPING FESTIVAL

Member U. S. E. A. S. A.

SATURDAY NIGHT, JUNE 1st
8:00 P.M.
Under Floodlights

20 CLUBS TO COMPETE

SUNDAY AFTERNOON, JUNE 2nd
2:00 P.M.

LAKE TELEMARK, ROCKAWAY, N. J.

SPONSORED BY
ODIN SKI CLUB
Sanctioned by U. S. E. A. S. A.

DONATION — 25 cents

Summer ski jumping brochure
Courtesy of Rockaway Township Library

LAKE TELEMARK

The Tokle family has a long history in the sport of ski jumping. Torger Tokle came from Norway and set the jump record on the famous ski jump at Bear Mountain, New York. There are reports that his jump record there of 180 feet was never broken. Torger was also a member of the 10th Mountain Division. He unfortunately died during World War II in Italy.

Art Tokle, Sr. also competed on the jumps in Bear Mountain and helped design and build the ski jumps at Lake Telemark as well as the ski jumps at the Craigmeur and Great Gorge South ski areas. Art Tokle, Sr. was the national jump champion in 1951 and 1953. He also competed in the 1952 Olympics. He made the Olympic team again in 1960. Rumor has it that he had a small ski jump set up in his backyard and that he continued to practice jumping. Art Tokle, Sr. passed away in March 2005.

Art Tokle, Jr. has continued in his family's footsteps in ski jumping history. He is currently the Chairman of the Eastern USSA Ski Jumping Committee.

Ski jumping ended in Lake Telemark in the 1960s. The Odin Ski Club unfortunately disbanded in the early 1980s due to lack of interest and lack of members.

Ellen (Skavnes) Tonnesen
Courtesy of Ellen (Skavnes) Tonnessen

Art Tokle, Sr. at Lake Telemark
Courtesy of Ellen (Skavnes) Tonnesen

LAKE TELEMARK

WELCOME SKI FANS
By
Arthur Tokle, President O. S. C.

In behalf of the Odin Ski Club, it is my pleasure to extend to all of you a very cordial welcome to our second annual ski jumping tournament here at the Odin Hill this weekend. Many of the top U. S. Ski Jumpers are again here to perform for you.

In presenting this tournament our club wishes to extend our most sincere appreciation to the newspapers, television studios, radio stations, and all others who have contributed to the success of this tournament.

The ski classics which you are about to see could not possibly be a success without the cooperation of you ski fans and to all of you we say—thank you.

PROGRAM:

EXHIBITION SKI JUMPING SATURDAY EVENING – 8:00 P.M.

Immediately following the ski jumping, a dance will be held at THE LAKE TELEMARK COUNTRY CLUB HOUSE.

ODIN SKI CLUB'S SPRING FESTIVAL TOURNAMENT
SUNDAY AFTERNOON – 2:00 P.M.

TROPHY DISTRIBUTION AT THE
LAKE TELEMARK COUNTRY CLUB HOUSE
SUNDAY EVENING – 7:00 P.M.

Classes are: A - B - C - and VETERANS
ANNOUNCER FOR ALL EVENTS IS: BILL (The Weasel) AVISON
From Greenfield, Mass.

Lake Telemark Summer ski jumping brochure - Courtesy of Rockaway Township Library

CHAPTER 24

MORGAN FARM SKI HILL
Route 23
Cedar Grove

Sledding sign on the old rope tow shack - Author's collection

In the late 18th Century the Canfield-Morgan house was built on a 14 acre farm in Cedar Grove. John and Susan Canfield originally owned the property. It was sold to J. Morgan in 1909. Reports show that the farm stayed in the Morgan family until 1985. J. Morgan died in 1985 and left the farm to the town of Cedar Grove to be preserved as open space. It was the last surviving farm in Essex County.

The farm site includes the Canfield-Morgan house, a recreational area with several short hills that are still used for sleigh riding, a small pond for ice skating, hiking trails, picnic areas and several small buildings.

The ski hill here opened in the early 1940s. The rope tow was built by using an engine from an old 1930s Ford Model A car. Skiing at this hill was always free. The tow shack and the old engine that ran the rope tow are still standing on the top of the old ski hill.

MORGAN FARM SKI HILL

There was only one short slope here. The area also included a small pond where visitors could also go ice skating.

The rope tow ceased operation in the 1960s. There may be a few beginner skiers that still use the hill, but if they want to take more runs they have to walk back up the slope.

The hill is still used today for sleigh riding.

Ski hill at Morgan Farm – Author's collection

Rope tow shack at Morgan Farm - Author's collection

CHAPTER 25

MT. BETHEL
Mansfield Township

Courtesy of Gene Weinmann (Mt. Bethel ski instructor)

The Mt. Bethel ski area opened in the 1960s. Some local residents remembered it only lasting a few years to some time in the mid 1970s.

George Meigs and John Conaghan were the operators of this ski hill. Members of their families also helped run Mt. Bethel. The slopes were located on the Upper Pohatcong Mountain range. The engines that ran the rope tows looked like they may have been made by Chrysler. Another car company that made rope tows and didn't know it!

Descriptions of the Mt. Bethel ski area included a small base lodge that had a ski shop and a snack bar. There was also a small pond on the property where people could go ice skating. Centenary College students were reported to have ice skated there regularly.

MT. BETHEL SKI AREA

Warming shack at the top of Mt. Bethel
Author's collection

Old slope at Mt. Bethel - Author's collection

There were only two slopes at this ski area. The vertical drop was only 195 feet. This small mountain had two rope tows and lights for night skiing.

Ski instructions were offered at the mountain. Jim Young was listed on a late 1960s information sheet as being the director of the ski school. Gene Weinmann was one of the ski instructors at the mountain.

Mt. Bethel had its own snow making equipment which was made by the owners.

In 1968 lift tickets were just $3.50 for adults and $2.50 for children. Lift tickets were around $5.00 a day in 1973.

Unfortunately this was one of the small New Jersey ski areas that only lasted a few years.
Mt. Bethel closed in the early 1970s.

MT. BETHEL SKI AREA

Chevy engines for rope tows - Author's collection

Rope tow pole - Author's collection

Rope tow remains - Author's collection

MT. BETHEL

Slopes and lodge - Courtesy of Gene Weinmann (Mt. Bethel ski instructor)

Winter at Mt. Bethel - Courtesy of Gene Weinmann (Mt. Bethel ski instructor)

View of lodge and slopes - Courtesy of Gene Weinmann

MT. BETHEL

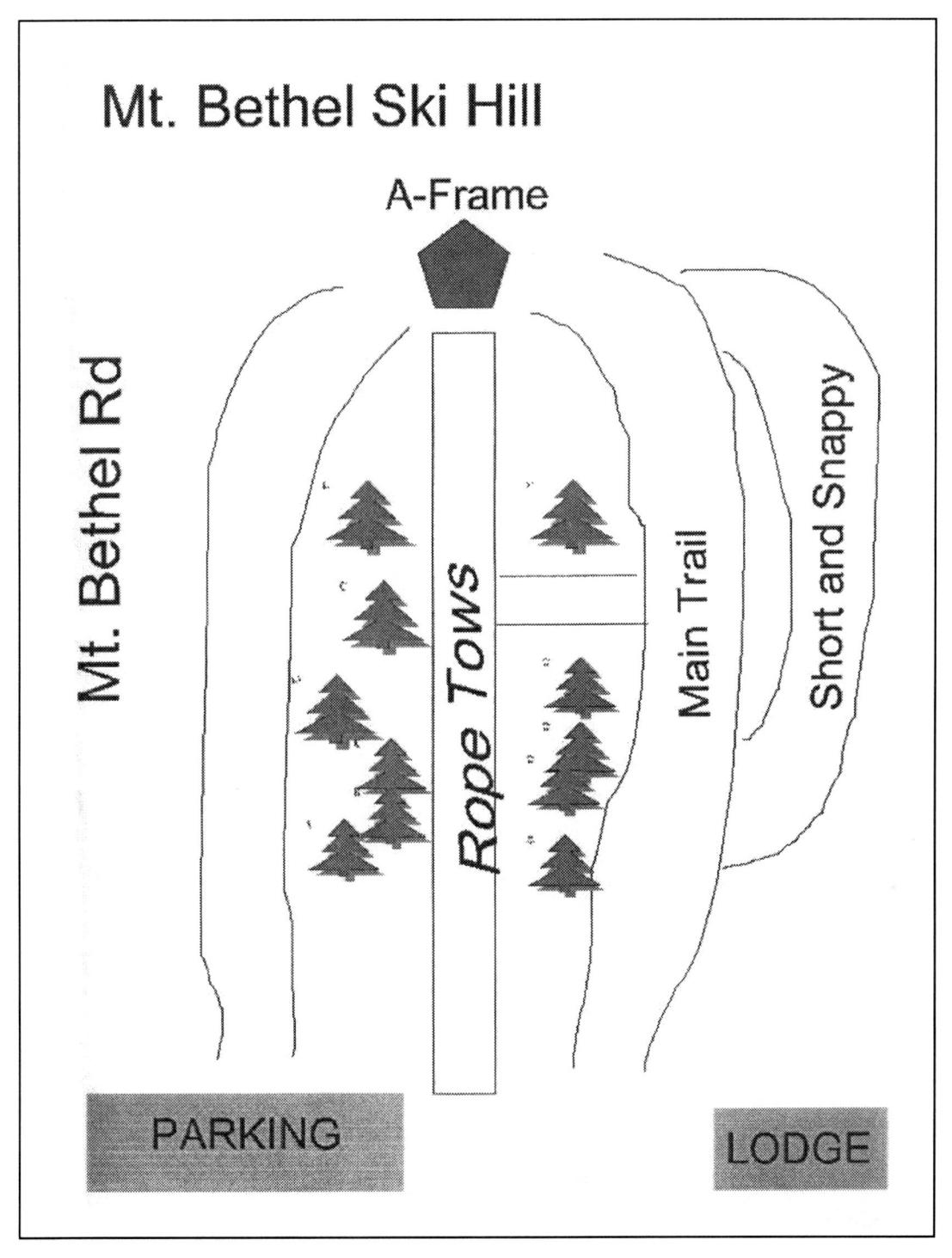

Map of Mt. Bethel Ski Area – Courtesy of Gene Weinmann (Mt. Bethel ski instructor)

MT. BETHEL SKI AREA

Gene Weinmann – Mt. Bethel ski instructor

CHAPTER 26

MOUNTAIN CREEK SKI AREA
Route 94
Vernon

Temporary lodge at Mountain Creek ski area – Author's collection

The Intrawest Company owns several major ski resorts in the United States and Canada. They purchased the Great Gorge South, Great Gorge North and Vernon Valley ski areas in 1998. The three ski areas were merged again into a new resort named Mountain Creek.

Intrawest made a lot of upgrades by installing new lighting, new chair lifts and redesigning some of the trails. There were also upgrades made to several of the old ski lodges. A Cabriolet gondola lift was put in at the Vernon Peak. It is the only gondola lift in New Jersey. The outside of the old Great Gorge South lodge has remained pretty much the same.
The inside underwent a total renovation.

In October 1999 a fire destroyed the original hexagon lodge at the old Vernon Valley ski area. Bubble type buildings were brought in as a temporary lodge and ski shop while a new lodge could be built. As of the winter of 2004 a new lodge still has not been built.

MOUNTAIN CREEK

Mountain Creek now encompasses 41 trails and 11 lifts. The vertical drop of the South side of Mountain Creek is 1,040 feet.

Mountain Creek's South Peak still has a dedicated ski racing trail. Many of the next potential famous ski racers are still getting their training there. There are also several terrain parks located at the new Mountain Creek resort. From a personal observation I feel that the new ski resort lost some of its charm when Intrawest decided to take out most of the chair lifts that ran to different parts of the mountain. There is no longer any mid station at any of the three peaks and all skiers now have to go to the top to ski down. When the three ski areas were originally built the owners put in several lifts that took you to different sections of the mountain. These lifts allowed skiers to take runs just at the bottom half of the mountain if that was what they wanted to do.

Entrance sign to Vernon base of Mountain Creek - Author's collection

MOUNTAIN CREEK

Slopes at Vernon base of Mountain Creek - Author's collection

New Jersey Transit and Mountain Creek have partnered up to provide bus service on the weekends direct from New York City. They are also looking into the possibility of reviving the ski trains that once ran out to the former Great Gorge South ski area.

Construction of a new condo/hotel at the Vernon base of Mountain Creek began during the winter of 2004/2005.

The Mountain Creek ski area is one of the few New Jersey ski areas that are still open.

CHAPTER 27

NEWTON SKI TOW
Route 519
Newton

Main slope at the Newton Ski Tow - Author's collection

This small ski area was located on a hillside directly across the road from the Sussex County Community College. You can still see a small trail that is about 8 feet wide running down the hill.

Clarence Wyker and Walt Mitchell opened the Newton Ski Tow on Bunker Hill in the 1940s. Clarence owned a small cattle ranch just up the road from the ski hill.

NEWTON SKI TOW

A local resident said that Clarence and his friends participated in many sports and really lived life to the fullest. The Roselli family owned the property where the ski hill was operated.

The Newton Ski Tow was in operation from the late 1940s to at least the early 1950s. A few Newton residents remembered people still skiing and sledding there in the 1960s. Descriptions I was given of the Newton Ski Tow included one open slope that was 1,200 feet long with a 375 foot vertical drop. There were also a 900 foot long rope tow and a small warming hut at the base of the ski hill. The ski area was only open on the weekends and holidays.
As small as this ski hill was, it did have a ski patrol. Unfortunately there was no snow making here and that was one reason it didn't operate for too long.

Rope tow pulley on top of telephone pole - Author's collection

NEWTON SKI TOW

Remains of small warming shack at bottom of slopes - Author's collection

Foundation for warming shack - Author's collection

CHAPTER 28

NORTH JERSEY COUNTRY CLUB – SKI JUMP
Hamburg Turnpike
Wayne

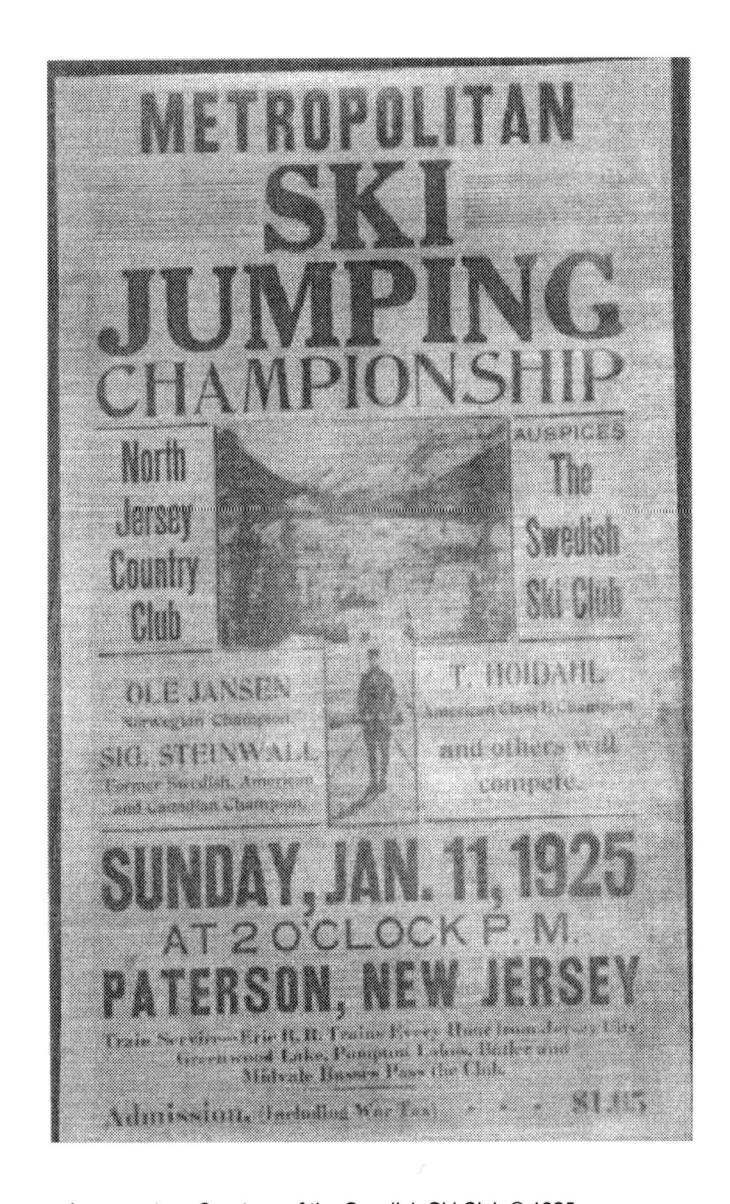

Jump poster - Courtesy of the Swedish Ski Club © 1925

This was probably the earliest ski jump built in New Jersey. It was also the first ski jump built in the metropolitan New York area. George Conradson and some other members of the Swedish Ski Club helped build the ski jump here in 1924. At that time people knew it as the Paterson Jump.

NORTH JERSEY COUNTRY CLUB JUMP

The first ski jumping tournament took place at the North Jersey Country Club on January 11, 1925. The Norsemen Ski Club was also reported to have participated in jump competitions here. The ski jump was used from 1925 until it was unfortunately destroyed by a storm in 1928.

Members of the Swedish Ski Club participated in many jump competitions held in the New Jersey and New York area.

The Swedish Ski Club also helped build the famous ski jump at the Bear Mountain State Park in New York. In 1928 they also sponsored the first ski jump tournament at Bear Mountain, New York. Their club continued to be a sponsor of it until 1990 when the ski jumps at Bear Mountain also closed.

FIRST SKI JUMPING TOURNAMENT NORTH JERSEY, C. C., JAN. 11, 1925
SIG STEINWALL, OUR FOUNDER, JUMPING

Courtesy of the Swedish Ski Club

CHAPTER 29

PEAPACK SKI AREA
Route 206
Peapack

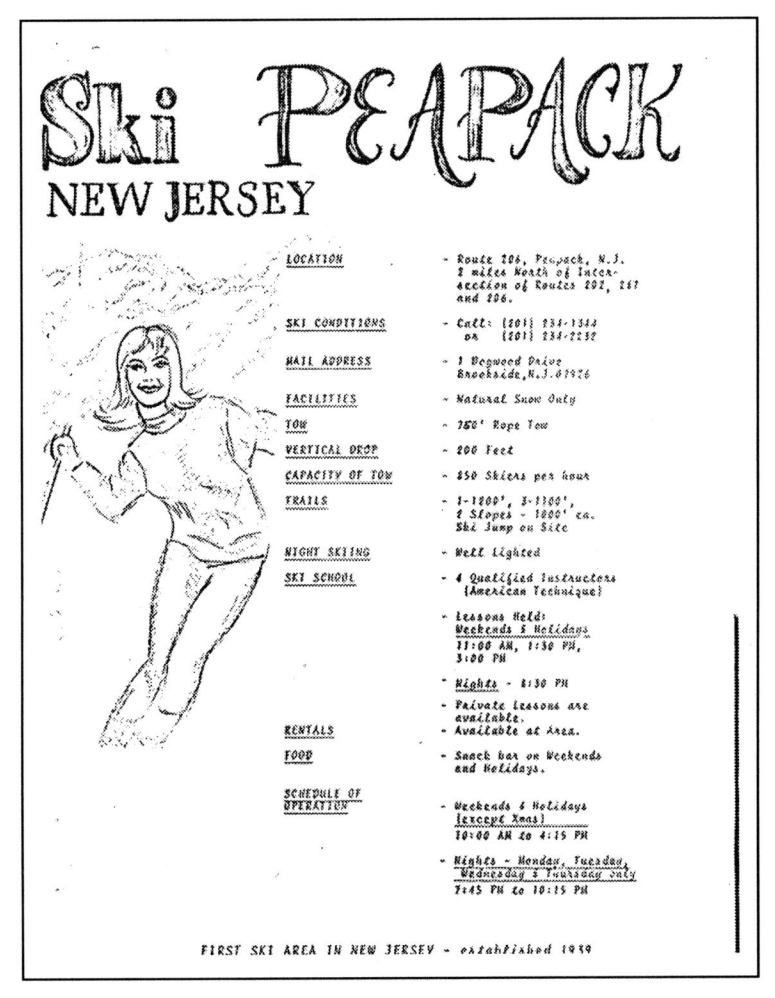

Brochure courtesy of the Peapack Library

In 1939 Melvyn Blaufuss and Gilbert Miller built their new ski area on Tiger's Hill. This property was used as a sheep meadow. The Peapack ski area was the second oldest in New Jersey. Running the ski hill was more of a hobby than a real business for Melvyn. Originally it was only open on week nights and weekends. When it first opened it was located on 20 acres of property on what was known at the time as Route 31. The road is now known as Route 206. Melvyn leased this property from its owners before he and Eric Hammerstorm purchased it in a tax sale in 1956.

PEAPACK SKI AREA

There were 4 trails at the mountain that were about 1,000 feet long. The vertical drop was only 200 feet. The rope tow was 700 feet long. A small ski jump was also located on the slopes.

Melvyn told me that he went to one of the New York state's ski areas to see their rope tow operation. Shortly after that he built his own tow. It was powered by an engine from a 1932 Oldsmobile.

The Lackawanna railroad ran a winter sports train that stopped at one of the train stations near Peapack's slopes. People who traveled to the ski area in cars parked them along the side of the highway.

Advertising brochures for the ski area were given out on the train stations and also in some of New York and New Jersey's largest department stores.

I heard reports that some famous people such as Jackie Kennedy and her children sometimes skied at the Peapack ski area.

The old slopes of the Peapack Ski Area – Author's collection   An old trail at Peapack – Author's collection

In the 1940s tickets for the ski area were $1.20 for a day or night, and were only $2.00 on weekends. People brought their lift tickets from Melvyn's wife, Christie, in the parking lot. Some snacks and refreshments were also sold from a small tent that was set up in the parking lot.

PEAPACK SKI AREA

If you wanted to rent equipment, you could get that from the back of a station wagon that Melvyn drove to the ski area. Peapack also rented ski gloves, because the speedy rope tow would sometimes rip through skier's gloves after a few rides.

The Princeton ski club frequented the Peapack Ski Area. There are reports that they set up a slalom race course and held several winter ski jump competitions on the slopes. They also held summer ski jumping competitions at the mountain on roller skis.

In the winter ski jumping was also a pretty popular sport at Peapack. Old listings showed that there were two ski jumps here. Melvyn Blaufuss told me that he would close the slopes every day around lunch time so the skiers could have break and also watch the jump competitions.

Princeton Ski Club Roller Skiing On The Hill
Summer 1972

Riding The Tow To The Top
(March 1964)

Pictures courtesy of the Peapack Library

Since there was no lodge at Peapack, many skiers packed their lunches and ate on the sides of the slopes while watching the daily ski jumping competitions. Some skiers brought beer with them and hid it on the slopes. Melvyn said there were lots of times when they forgot where they hid it, so he and the other workers at Peapack would end up with some free beer.

PEAPACK SKI AREA

Unfortunately there was no snow making equipment here. The owners also couldn't afford the increasing insurance premiums. In 1987 the Peapack ski area closed for good.

In 1989 a small housing development was built near the site of the old ski slopes. Part of the old slopes can still be seen, however, they are now on private property. There are two private houses on the former Peapack ski slopes.

Peapack Ski Area patch
Courtesy of Peapack Library

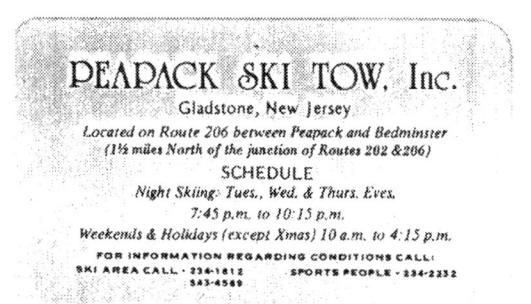

Business card from Peapack Ski Area
Courtesy of Peapack Library

Ticket from Peapack Ski Area
Courtesy of Peapack Library

CHAPTER 30

PINE NEEDLE SLOPE
Route 521
Swartswood Lake

Erling Omland at the Pine Needle Slope
Courtesy of Erling Omland

Rope tow at the Pine Needle Slope
Courtesy of Erling Olmand

This unique ski slope opened in 1938 at the Rustic R Ranch. The story of this ski slope says that Eugene Riss wanted to have something on his property from his home country of France. Thick layers of pine needles were put down on the slopes so people could ski all year long. Large trucks were used to bring in pine needles from the local area. Layers of the pine needles about 6 inches deep were spread over the slope. The only grooming equipment here was a few people that stood on the side of the slope and raked the needles back on to the slope after the skiers took their runs.

PINE NEEDLE SLOPE

Some early well known New Jersey skiers like Erling Omland and Arnie Kirbach, Sr., from the Watchung Ski Club, participated in ski jumping and racing tournaments that were held there. Both of them remembered the slope as being really dirty and dusty.

```
COMPETITION        by    James M. Spees
     To talk of pine needle skiing after we have skied on our
first and second snowfalls seems as inappropriate as a discus-
sion of last summer's fishing trips---but to keep this report
complete a summary of the November 17th Pine Needle meet at the
Rustic R Dude Ranch is necessary. For the sake of brevity we
report only the prize winners and the Watchung skiers.
                       DOWNHILL                              Total
 1. James Carew, New York Ski Club        11.6    11.4       23.0
 2. Erling Omland, Watchung               11.6    11.6       23.2
 3. Matt Nuttila, New York Ski Club       12.0    11.8       23.8
 4. Fritz Lunde, Watchung   (3 way tie)   12.0    12.0       24.0
 5. Richard Wade,   "       (2 way tie)   12.2    12.0       24.2
 6. Walter Stocker, "                     12.4    12.0       24.4
 9. James Spees &   "                     12.8    12.8       25.6
    Ted Pistor     "                      12.2    13.4       25.6
15. Arnold Kirbach, "                     12.0    20.0       32.0
18. Hoddy Beazlie,  "                     29.0    12.6       41.6
     The slow times of the last two runners were due to beau-
tiful sitzmarks which they carved in the needles. I wonder if
it felt anything like a hot-foot?
                       JUMPING           (20% Penalty for fall)
 1. Heinz Krebs, New York Ski Club       54-6 (Pen)  55-11   99-5
 2. Arnold Kirbach, Watchung             46-0        48-0 (Pen) 84-4
 3. Erling Omland,  "                    40-3        41-9    82-0
 7. Fritz Lunde,    "                    40-8 (Pen)  39-8    72-2
```

Pine Needle Slope competition results
Courtesy of Erling Omland – Watchung Ski Club

Other ski clubs such as the Swedish Ski Club and the New York Ski Club also participated in various events held here. Erling and Arnie said that skiers tried many different things to wax their skis so they would have an easier time skiing down the slope. Some waxed their long wood skis by dipping them in long pans that had a carpet on the bottom of it and was filled with kerosene. Most skiers found that this worked the best to keep their skis from sticking to the pine needles.

Arnie said that there was a pan at the bottom so you could dip your skis into before going up the rope tow. Another one was located at the top so you could "wax" your skis again before taking your run down the pine needle slope. The Pine Needle Slope was mostly used during the off season, but it was used during the winter when there was enough snow.

This unique New Jersey ski slope closed down in the early 1940s. The Pine Needle Slope was located property that is now known as the Girl Scout's Camp Lou Henry Hoover. The Girl Scouts purchased the property in 1953 and have owned it since.

CHAPTER 31

ROCK VIEW HOTEL
River Road
Montague

Rock View Hotel
Courtesy of Alicia Batko - Montague Association for Restoration of Community History (M.A.R.C.H.)

In the late 1930s the Rock View Hotel had a small ski hill. The Rock View was one of the locations that people could easily reach by taking the early "Snow King" ski trains from Jersey City, New Jersey to Port Jervis, New York.

Promotional brochures from the 1930s talk about the hotel being nestled on the Delaware River and having skiing, tobogganing and skating available for their guests during the winter season. There were no rope tows at this ski hill. For added entertainment the Rock View also had a casino. The hotel's brochures also noted that anyone looking for some steeper slopes and a professional ski jump could go to the High Point State Park which was only 5 miles from the hotel.

ROCK VIEW

$13.50 covered the cost of the train ride from New York City to Port Jervis, New York, your weekend lodging and meals at the Rock View Hotel, and skiing there.

It's been said that the famous actor Roy Rogers even took trips to Rock View and also brought his famous horse with him. When Roy was staying there and enjoying some skiing – the employees were not allowed to tell anyone that he was there.

The Rock View Hotel was last known as the Rock View Golf Club. The State of New Jersey recently purchased the property.

Ad from Erie Snow Train brochure © 1936
Courtesy of (M.A.R.C.H.) Montague Association for Restoration of Community History

From Rock View Inn booklet – Courtesy of (M.A.R.C.H.) Montague Association for Restoration of Community History

CHAPTER 32

SKI MOUNTAIN
Branch Avenue & DeCou Road
Pine Hill

Beginner ski lessons at Ski Mountain - Old magazine photo © 1960s

Emil DelConte, John Early and Ed Klumpp were the driving forces behind this ski area. They were all local residents who loved to ski and wanted to share that with others. Ski Mountain was open for over 20 years. It was only about 15 minutes away from Philadelphia, Pennsylvania.

You wouldn't think that there would be any hills in Pine Hill that would be steep enough to build a ski slope on, but these men found one. In 1964 Ski Mountain opened on the steepest hill in the town that was 209 feet tall. Some reports said that from the top of the ski resort you could see the nearby town of Clementon.

When I talked with Emil DelConte, he told me that he, John and Ed did a lot of research into the ski industry before they opened their ski area. They also found that the weather in Pine Hill seemed to be pretty favorable for them to open a ski area there. They were also smart to invest in some snow making and grooming equipment right from the beginning so they could keep their ski slopes in good shape.

There were 4 trails with 1 t-bar, 2 pomas and 2 rope tows. The vertical drop of the steepest slope was 137 feet.

SKI MOUNTAIN

Ski Mountain's main slope - Picture from The Evening Bulletin – Feb. 3, 1978

Emil DelConte told me that there was a small lodge at the bottom of the slopes. It was also reported that Danzeisen & Quigley also ran a ski shop in the lodge.

Ski Mountain had over 100 ski instructors. Neal Robinson from Glen Ellen, Vermont ran their ski school. After the Vietnam War they had a special amputee ski program at the mountain that became extremely popular.
This gave the Vets something to do to try to keep their minds off what they had been through during the War. The ski patrollers at this mountain were also part of the National Ski Patrol system.

The three owners of Ski Mountain were also members of the New Jersey Ski Areas Association. They were driving forces in much of the legislation that was passed in New Jersey on how the state's ski areas would be run.

In the early 1980s, the owners of Ski Mountain went into a partnership with the Great American Recreation Company. They opened a small summer amusement and water park called Action Park at Ski Mountain. The Great American Recreation Company also operated another Action Park at the Vernon Valley ski area in Vernon. There were many similar action rides at Ski Mountain that were also at the Vernon Valley ski area.

SKI MOUNTAIN

Unfortunately there were many financial difficulties at the ski area. Ski Mountain was forced into bankruptcy in 1986. Shortly after that a fire that burned down the ski lodge.

The ski area property sat empty for many years until a new world-class golf course was built on the site in 1999.

The new Pine Hill Golf Club – formerly Ski Mountain - Author's collection

Ski Mountain patch – Author's collection    Pine Hill Golf Course – Author's collection

CHAPTER 33

SNOW BOWL
Weldon Road
Milton

Snow Bowl sign courtesy of anonymous skiers

Frank Johnson opened the Snow Bowl ski area in 1962. I was told that Mr. Johnson was a psychiatrist who lived in Princeton. The ski area was located on 200 acres on the slopes of Bowling Green Mountain.

Snow Bowl was located next to a local elementary school and a high school. Some friends told me that they used to skip some classes to go out and take a few runs on the slopes. I was also told that if you knew someone's ski style and they cut class, you could look out the windows of the school and you could pick them out on Snow Bowl's slopes. The kids also walked over there after school was over to also get some runs in before going home.

Snow Bowl was another ski area that started out small. It had just one rope tow in the beginning. There were 7 full time Austrian ski instructors as well as around 30 part time ski instructors at the mountain.

SNOW BOWL

Descriptions of the ski lodge tell that it was another one that started out small and grew over the years. From around 1966 to 1969 the ski area went through several expansions.

After the expansions, Snow Bowl had 7 trails and 4 open slopes. There were 2 chair lifts, 3 t-bars and 2 rope tows that carried skiers to the top of the runs. The expanded ski lodge had three levels with several restaurants. Roy Scovill said that the lodge also had a replicated 17th Century bar in the basement called the "Rusty Hinge Tavern". It was complete with saw dust on the floor and old ski equipment hanging on the walls. The bar also brought in live entertainment such as the "Hudson River Burial Society". The lodge also had a heated outdoor swimming pool. In the summer there were also tennis courts located near the lodge.

Ownership of the ski area changed several times during the late 1960s and early 1970s. Several managers of Snow Bowl included Ed Lapinter from around 1963 to 1966, Ralph Laschont from 1966 to 1968, and Roy Scovill from 1968 to 1970. Ed Lapinter also ran the ski school.

Unfortunately like some of the other ski resorts, Snow Bowl went bankrupt and closed in 1973. I was told that when the ski area closed, all of their equipment was sold off to other local New Jersey ski areas. The double chair lift on the Chicken Delight slope at the Hidden Valley ski area, as well as the tables and chairs from the restaurant and bar were also sold to Hidden Valley. About 3 years after the resort closed, a fire destroyed the ski lodge.

Snow Bowl ski patch – Author's collection

SNOW BOWL

Snow Bowl ski area pictures courtesy of Joe Trezza © 1960s

Snow Bowl closed down long before the Morris County Parks Department bought the land in 1986. There is not much left of the old ski area except for a few old chair lift bull wheels and some foundations of the old buildings that were there.

There have been several proposals to try to reopen the Snow Bowl ski area over the years, but so far nothing has happened with any of them. Could the Snow Bowl ski area reopen again? Only time will tell.

Making snow on Snow Bowl's slopes
Courtesy of Joe Trezza © 1960s

SNOW BOWL

An old ski trail. It is still used today by skiers and snowboarders who hike up the mountain.

Author's collection

Rusty remains of an old chair lift.

Author's collection

CHAPTER 34

SUCCASUNNA SKI AREA
Pleasant Hill Road
Succasunna

Erling Omland from the Watchung Ski Club gave me some wonderful information about this little ski hill. It showed that it was operated by Herb and Madeline Fatum. Unfortunately the exact date it opened was not listed. I did find several listings of it from the 1940s.

This ski area was located on a hill at the Succasunna Golf Club. There was 1 trail with 1 rope tow. It only offered skiing when there was enough natural snow. The descriptions of the ski hill also included a ski jump.

The slope was used for golf in the off season. A housing development was built on the site of this old ski area in the early 1960s. Unfortunately not much else is known about this short lived ski hill.

CHAPTER 35

SUSSEX SKI TOW
Lewisburg Road
Lewisburg (Sussex)

Spreen's ski hill - Author's Collection

The Sussex Ski Tow was located on the Spreen family's dairy farm. Besides owning the dairy farm and operating the ski hill in the winter, the family also owned a small dry goods store in Sussex. The Upsala College's Sussex campus was located near this ski hill.

This small ski hill operated from around 1947 through the late 1950s. There are reports that it possibly operated even into the early 1960s. Some local residents I spoke to all had fond memories of skiing on this slope. A few people told me they remembered this slope being called Spreen's Ski Tow. I was told that skiers were sometimes brought to the hill by a horse drawn sleigh when there was too much snow on the roads for the cars to get there.

Descriptions of the Sussex Ski Tow included 1 beginner slope with a 250 foot rope tow, 1 advanced slope with a 1,250 foot rope tow, and a small warming hut. This slope was only open on the weekends and holidays from around 9:30am to dusk. Tickets for the rope tow were only $2.00.

SUSSEX SKI TOW

Old Ford Model A engines were located at the top of the slopes which ran the rope tows. A horse rope was used for the rope tows and it was run through wheels that were suspended on top of some tall poles. This was another one of New Jersey's short lived ski hills.

Spreen's ski hill - Author's collection

CHAPTER 36

THOMPSON PARK
Forsgate Drive
Jamesburg

Ski lodge at Thompson Park – Courtesy of Doug Kiovsky

The Thompson Park Ski Center opened in 1964. The Middlesex County Parks Department ran the ski hill. Bob Cash was the director of the Parks Department at that time.

A friend told me that people used the hill for sledding long before the ski center was opened. He also told me that the slope was referred to "Devil's Hill'. When the ski hill opened a fence was put up between the sledding hill and the ski hill so there wouldn't be any serious accidents.

The ski center was located on 9 acres in Thompson Park. The vertical drop of the slope was 135 feet. There was a small lodge at the base of the ski slope. It had a fireplace, snack bar, and a small rental shop. Thompson Park's Ski Center had 1 ski instructor.

The slopes here also had lights for night skiing. One person told me that there was a blinking light at the bottom of the hill that told you when the rope tow was going to close for the evening.

THOMPSON PARK SKI CENTER

Admission was only $0.50 in 1968 and $1.50 in 1973. The ski area was closed in the 1980s after some kind of unfortunate accident happened on the slopes. It's been reported that the hill is still used by kids for sleigh riding.

Main slope at Thompson Park Ski Center – Courtesy of Doug Kiovsky

Old ski lodge and no toboggans or no snow boarding sign.
Courtesy of Doug Kiovsky.

CHAPTER 37

THUNDER MOUNTAIN SKI AREA
Shepherd Lake
Ringwood

Remains of the main slope at Thunder Mountain - Author's collection

The Prince and Loomis families were wealthy families who lived in the Ringwood area. They both originally owned some of the property at Shepherd Lake in the 1800s.

A 1970s newspaper article said that the Shepherd Lake area was operated as a private country club before the state bought the property in 1964 with Green Acres money. A local resident remembers that there was skiing at Thunder Mountain in 1955.

Local residents said that this ski area was also known as Eagle Mountain. There was a high profile court case in 1964 because of a disagreement between another ski resort also named Thunder Mountain over the use of the name.

THUNDER MOUNTAIN

The Thunder Mountain ski resort in Massachusetts took the New Jersey ski area to court because they felt that when ski reports were given people wouldn't know which Thunder Mountain's conditions were being reported. The Massachusetts resort lost the court case and they were both able to use the Thunder Mountain name.

This ski area had its own three level lodge. It was also used in the off season to host many weddings and parties. Unfortunately the original lodge burned down in the 1970s after the ski hill closed.

There was 1 double chair lift and 2 T-bars here. The mountain also had several ski instructors.

A 1964 listing shows that lift tickets were $3.25 for adults on the week days and $3.95 on weekends and holidays. Besides the ski runs at Thunder Mountain, the area had many other recreational opportunities available like ice skating, swimming and boating as well as hiking.

Skiing ended here in the early 1970s. Unfortunately the original lodge burned down after the ski area closed.

The hillside is now pretty much grown over, but if you know where to look you can still find remnants of the old ski area.

A new recreation lodge was built at Shepherd Lake in the early 1980s.

Remains of one of the rope tows - Author's collection

THUNDER MOUNTAIN

The Shepherd Lake area is still used today by many boaters and swimmers. Fishing is also allowed at the lake. There are also many hiking trails that surround the area.

Thunder Mountain skeet shooting club still operates at the top of the old ski slopes. Thunder Mountain and Shepherd Lake are part of the Ringwood State Park System.

Remains of old bull wheel – Author's collection

Remains of lift poles - Author's collection

THUNDER MOUNTAIN

Remains of old rope tow – Author's collection

Thunder Mountain advertisements
(Also known as Eagle Mountain)

Remains of old ski run and snow fencing – Author's collection

CHAPTER 38

VERNON SKI TOW
Drew Mountain Road & Route 517
Vernon Township

Open slope at the Vernon Ski Tow - Courtesy of Ted Hine © 1940s – 1950s

Ted Hine was very young when his father built the Vernon Ski Tow in the Vernon Valley. Most of his memories of the ski hill came from older relatives telling him stories of their experiences there. He was fortunate enough though to have a lot of pictures and information about the Vernon Ski Tow passed down to him. Ted has graciously allowed me to tell the story of this ski hill.

Kirt Hine, Ted's father, was a ski racer at Yale University from 1935 to 1939. He was ranked second in downhill and slalom during his racing career. After college, Kirt became a designer for the Propeller Division of the Curtiss-Wright Company. During World War II he was a member of the Army's famous 10th Mountain Division.

VERNON SKI TOW

Kirt Hine, Bill McKelvy and Woody Walker all worked for the Curtiss-Wright Company in Fairfield, New Jersey as well as operating the Vernon Ski Tow on weekends. They opened this ski hill because they loved to ski and wanted to share that with others.

The Chardavyone family owned the property on Pochuck Mountain where the Vernon Ski Tow was built. Kirt Hine and Bill McKelvy did a lot of searching by car and by air plane during 1945 before they found the site where they built their ski hill. They spent the rest of the year of 1945 clearing the 22 acres for their new slopes and building the warming shack and the rope tow.

The Vernon Ski Tow was one of the earliest ski hills in the Vernon Valley. Old promotional sheets about this ski slope said that there were signs along Route 23 in Stockholm and Hamburg to help lead skiers to this location.

Warming shack - Courtesy of Ted Hine © 1940s – 1950s

VERNON SKI TOW

Descriptions of this ski area included several wide open slopes. The longest trail was 1,500 feet. There was a small warming shack at the top of the slopes.

Kirt and Bill's wives also worked at the ski hill selling hot drinks and snacks in the small warming shack. Woody Walker was the ski patroller at the mountain.

Woody told me the story of how he met his wife, Carlee, on the slopes of their ski hill. "I was on the hill near the warming shack when this pretty young girl came down the hill and blooped it, head over heels into a snow bank not far from where I was standing."

"I went over and pulled her out and after she dusted the snow off her face, she looked at me with a fantastic smile. I asked her how she felt and she agreed she was a bit shaken up and suggested that we meet down at the shed and talk. That was it."

"She lived in Boston and was visiting friends that lived in West Caldwell, New Jersey. I didn't have a car and we agreed to drive home together. That was my first contact with the girl who would later become my wife. We got together a number of times after that, and in June I proposed to her. On September 29 we were married in New York City. We bought a little house in Packanack Lake, New Jersey and had almost 50 years together before she passed away in 1996."

Skiers on the slopes of the Vernon Ski Tow – Courtesy of Ted Hine

VERNON SKI TOW

Since the owners of the Vernon Ski Tow all had regular jobs at the Curtiss-Wright Company, they only operated the ski hill on weekends and holidays. They would pack up their cars and drive from North Caldwell to the ski hill in Vernon Township. When they arrived, they would set up the car on the slopes and take the tires off and install the wooden wheels they built to run the rope tow. When the day was done, they would put the tires back on the car and drive it home.

Courtesy of Ted Hine © 1940s – 1950s

The Vernon Ski Tow closed in the early 1950s. This ski hill may have been short lived, but it gave thousands of people from the New York area many hours of fun skiing.

VERNON SKI TOW

Skiers preparing to ride back up the rope tow - Courtesy of Ted Hine © 1940s – 1950s

On the slopes at the Vernon Ski Tow - Courtesy of Ted Hine © 1940s – 1950s

VERNON SKI TOW

Riding up the rope tow - Courtesy of Ted Hine © 1940s – 1950s

Another ride up the rope tow - Courtesy of Ted Hine © 1940s – 1950s

CHAPTER 39

VERNON VALLEY SKI AREA
Route 94
Vernon

Author's collection

The Vernon Valley ski area was built on Hamburg Mountain in 1968. George Lupo was the original owner. Otto Schneibs designed trails at many ski resorts and was brought in to help design the slopes here.

This new ski area had a beautiful 300 foot long hexagon shaped ski lodge with large windows that faced the slopes. Inside there was a small ski shop, a cafeteria, a restaurant and the Hexagon Lounge bar. There were 12 trails with 6 chair lifts and 1 rope tow.

Some very unique events were held on the slopes of the ski area. One of them was a canoe race in the early 1970s. Each team brought their own canoes to the mountain to run them down the courses that were set up on the ski slopes.

There were also events like a beer slalom race where each participant had to stop and drink a beer at certain points before finishing their run. Other events included events known as pond skimming.

VERNON VALLEY

This mountain had 15 internationally certified full time ski instructors as well as 25 part time instructors available to give lessons every day.

During the 1970s most of the ski areas in New Jersey as well as some other areas experienced financial difficulties. Other forces like the 1970s energy crunch, high insurance costs and a lack of snow forced the ski area to close down for a time. New financing was put together that allowed the ski area to continue to operate.

The Great American Recreation Company opened what they called the Action Park at Vernon Valley during the late 1970s. One of the most popular attractions was the Alpine Slide. It was a cement track built into the side of one of the slopes. People would sit on top of a plastic cart that had a hand brake and speed down the windy cement track. Unfortunately many people ended up with scratched arms and legs if they didn't keep them inside the cart.

Other rides included a huge sling shot ride, a bungie type ride, water slides, mini race cars, and other various outdoor adventure rides. The Vernon Valley ski area also played host to many festivals and concerts in the off season.

Vernon Valley closed in 1997. It was open for over 30 years.
The main lodge at the former Vernon Valley ski area burned down in a fire in October 1999.

The ski area was sold to the Intrawest Company in 1998. Intrawest made many upgrades by installing new lifts, new lighting and upgrading the snow making equipment. They reopened the resort in 1999 under the new name of Mountain Creek.

VERNON VALLEY

Author's collection

Author's collection

Author's collection

159

VERNON VALLEY

Old trail map of Vernon Valley

CHAPTER 40

PROPOSED SKI AREAS

Over the years there have been several proposals for ski areas throughout New Jersey. Unfortunately some of them didn't come to fruition.

APPLE ACRES - In 1965 there was a proposal for a ski area to be built at Apple Acres in West Milford. The plans included several trails from 1,500 to 1,800 feet long with a vertical of 250 feet. A rope tow that was going to be 550 feet long was in the plans as well as snow making equipment and a shop for rental equipment. It was going to be operated by Ehlen Terhune and Gilbert L. Terhune, Jr. This ski hill never opened.

MOUNT JUNK - In the West Berlin area near Toms River a ski slope was going to be built on a garbage dump. Ski jumps, toboggan runs and rope tows or chair lifts were also included in the plans. An early name that was considered was to call it Mount Junk. Unfortunately it was decided that having a ski hill made out of a garbage dump was not a good idea.

SKI TRAILS U.S.A. - In the 1960s a plan was submitted for a ski hill near Atlantic City. It was going to be called Ski Trails U.S.A. Robert Kronowitz wanted to build a ski tower that would have been 250 feet high.

Descriptions of it included three ski runs. The runs would be on aluminum and would also have snow making equipment. A movable sidewalk was going to serve as a lift. Elevators in the towers would also take the more advanced skiers to the very top of the runs.

The plans also included a lounge and snack bar at the top. A skating rink was proposed to be built at the bottom of the runs as well as a ski lodge, a ski shop and refreshment area. SKI TRAILS U.S.A. never opened.

UNTERMEYER SKI CENTER - In the late 1960s there was a proposal to build a small ski resort in Kinnelon on the former Untermeyer Estate. The Gilbreth family had plans to build a winter resort area there until a fire destroyed the beautiful mansion in 1968. The ski and winter resort was never built. After standing empty for almost 3 decades, the former Untermeyer Estate house was purchased several years ago. It is being restored to its former glory by its new owner.

PROPOSED SKI AREAS

WALLPACK SKI CENTER – The builders of the Great Gorge ski area planned to build another ski area in the late 1960s. This new ski area would have been in the Tocks Island Recreation area near Wallpack Center. It was to be built on a slope near Tillman's Ravine on the Kittatinny ridge. A lodge, ski trails, and lifts were all in the proposal. This ski area would have encompassed 800 acres. It was never built.

XANADU SNOWDOME - There is a proposal for New Jersey's first indoor ski area scheduled to be built at the Meadowlands area. A complete sports, entertainment and educational complex will be built there. The indoor ski center will be part of the Xanadu proposal. Plans include a ski lodge, trails, lifts and indoor snow making. This indoor ski center could be the first one in the United States. It is scheduled to be open some time in 2006. Only time will tell if this one actually happens.

Who knows maybe some day someone will submit a proposal to re-open one of New Jersey's ski areas that closed. I think trying to reopen some of the old ones would be really great.

There may have been more proposed ski areas that were never built. No one knows for sure exactly how many more ski areas could have been built in New Jersey.

CHAPTER 41

THE FUTURE

Remains of old bull wheel - Author's collection

What's in the future for the sport of skiing and snow boarding in New Jersey? Only time will tell. Will some of the old ski areas reopen? Will any new ski areas be built in New Jersey? Will the sport of skiing and snow boarding in our state just fade away for good?

The people who opened the first ski areas in the state were skiers who wanted to share their enjoyment of the sport. Unfortunately almost all of New Jersey's ski hills are now long gone and only survive in the memories of the people who skied at them.

We have come a long way from using those long wood skis and short leather boots. New Jersey's ski areas have grown tremendously from those first short hills that were scattered on various farms and hillsides where skiers had to walk back up to take their next run down.

THE FUTURE

Skier at the Vernon Ski Tow – Courtesy of Ted Hine © 1940s – 1950s

Changes are constantly being made to the ski and snowboard equipment we are all using.

For a state like New Jersey that many would not really consider being a ski mecca, it is incredible that our state has had so much ski history!

There is a long history of skiing in New Jersey from the early 1920s to the present. Our little "ski state" should be proud. Many unique ski events happened over the years. Our state even produced several World Cup and Olympic champions, as well as many famous ski jumpers.

THE FUTURE

There was much to offer in the winter sport of skiing in our state and there still is.

There are only three alpine ski areas still open in the state. They are Campgaw Mountain in Mahwah and Hidden Valley and Mountain Creek in Vernon.

I can only hope that the few ski areas left in our state will be able to survive for many years to come. Maybe there will be more people that can say they learned to ski in New Jersey!

Next time someone laughs at you for skiing in New Jersey you can tell them just how many ski slopes there were in the state.

Ski sign - Author's collection

REFERENCES

ARROWHEAD SKI AREA

Arrowhead Ski Area – brochure

Arrowhead Ski Area – Dedication – December 17, 1978

Inner tube tobogganing - Asbury Park Press - 2/8/1985

Marlboro Township Recreation & Parks

Monmouth County Historical Society

New Jersey Ski Areas – New Jersey Department of Conservation (1968)

New Jersey Ski Areas – New Jersey Division of Economic Development (1972)

New Jersey Ski Areas – New Jersey Department of Conservation (1973)

News Tribune newspaper articles

Remembering the 20th Century – An Oral History of Monmouth County
    June West interview 6/19/2000 – Monmouth County Library

The Ski Industry – New Jersey Business – November 1974

YMCA Camp Arrowhead office

YMCA Camp Arrowhead – website

BELLE MOUNTAIN

Belle's future lifted
    Trenton Times – 9/22/1990

Belle Mountain Ski Area – brochure

Call it "Bare Mountain"
    Trenton Times – 1/3/1987

Keeping ski area open a battle
    Trenton Times – 1988

Lacking operator, Belle slopes closed
    Trenton Times – 11/5/1998

New Jersey Ski Areas – New Jersey Department of Conservation (1964)

New Jersey Ski Areas – New Jersey Department of Conservation (1968)

New Jersey Ski Areas – New Jersey Division of Economic Development (1972)

BELLE MOUNTAIN

New Jersey Ski Areas – New Jersey Department of Conservation (1973)
Snow job set for Belle Mountain
    Trenton Times – 12/10/1993

The Ski Industry – New Jersey Business – November 1974

Warm winter weather bares Belle Mountain
    Trenton Times – 12/28/1984

BERTHIAUME'S

Alicia Batko – Montague Association for the Restoration of Community History (M.A.R.C.H.)

Jeannie Sweetman – The Herald News

CAMPGAW MOUNTAIN

Campgaw Mountain brochures

Campgaw Offers Family Fun
    The Record – 2/24/1994

Campgaw Park Will Preserve Rugged Beauty Of The Area
    Mahwah Enterprise – 11/12/1955

Campgaw skiing – no need to sit on frozen assets
    Home and Store News – 2/7/1996

Cold War at Campgaw Mountain
    by Donald E. Bender - Bergen County Historical Society web site

New Jersey Ski Areas – New Jersey Department of Conservation (1968)

New Jersey Ski Areas – New Jersey Division of Economic Development (1972)

New Jersey Ski Areas – New Jersey Department of Conservation (1973)

Ski Slopes Get Good Use
    Home and Store News – 12/9/1970

Skiing The Hills Of Home – Thrills In Your Own Back Yard
    by: Allen Macaulay – The Record – January 16. 1994

The Ski Industry – New Jersey Business – November 1974

Snow works Bergen magic
    The Record – 1/13/1976

CAMPGAW MOUNTAIN

Start Developing Park In Mahwah
  Mahwah Enterprise – 3/17/1956

CAMP MIDVALE

Claude Ballester – National Ski Patrol – New Jersey Division

North Jersey Highlands Historical Society

Ringwood Township web page

Weis Center
  by Maureen Woop – The Trends – 3/2/1994

Weis Ecology Center - 2/20/2002

CRAIGMEUR SKI AREA

Craigmeur Ski Area brochure – 1988/1989

Craigmeur Ski Area – Newfoundland, New Jersey

Dorothy Murray – phone interview
  Owner - Craigmeur Recreation Area

New Jersey Ski Areas – New Jersey Department of Conservation (1964)

New Jersey Ski Areas – New Jersey Department of Conservation (1968)

New Jersey Ski Areas – New Jersey Division of Economic Development (1972)

New Jersey Ski Areas – New Jersey Department of Conservation (1973)

Prosperity On The Down Slopes – New Jersey Business – January 1967

Ray Schank – personal interviews
  General Manager – Craigmeur Recreation Area

Skiing The Hills Of Home – Thrills In Your Own Back Yard
  By: Allen Macaulay – The Record – January 16, 1994

The Ski Industry – New Jersey Business – November 1974

Art Tokle, Jr. – personal interview

World Ski Book – edited by Frank Elkins & Frank Harper - 1949

GALLOPING HILL SKI CENTER

To Benefit The Whole Population
    From: Union County Parks Commission

New Jersey Ski Areas – New Jersey Department of Conservation (1964)

New Jersey Ski Areas – New Jersey Department of Conservation (1968)

New Jersey Ski Areas – New Jersey Division of Economic Development (1972)

New Jersey Ski Areas – New Jersey Department of Conservation (1973)

The Ski Industry – New Jersey Business – November 1974

World Ski Book – edited by Frank Elkins & Frank Harper - 1949

GREAT GORGE NORTH

Areas Best Ski Slopes Being Built
    Herald News – July 22, 1971

Ray Bolger - interviews

Great Gorge North/South brochure 1972-1973

Great Gorge north plans revealed
    Photo News – 9/13/1970

Great Gorge North Plans Reviewed
    New Jersey Herald – 8/27/1970

The Ski Industry – New Jersey Business – November 1974

GREAT GORGE SOUTH

Ray Bolger - interviews

Great Gorge North/South brochure 1972-1973

Great Gorge Slates Ski Racing Program
    North Jersey Photo News – 12/6/1970

Jet Engine Produces Snow and More Snow

Kurlander forecasts "great growth" for area
    North Jersey Photo News – 10/15/1970

Laud Great Gorge Jet Snowmaker – 3/12/1970

New Jersey Ski Areas – New Jersey Department of Conservation (1968)

GREAT GORGE SOUTH

New Jersey Ski Areas – New Jersey Division of Economic Development (1972)

New Jersey Ski Areas – New Jersey Department of Conservation (1973)

Prosperity On The Down Slopes – New Jersey Business – January 1967

Ski Industry Transforms Vernon's Farming Face
    Herald News – 3/2/1971

Skiing The Hills Of Home – Thrills In Your Own Back Yard
    By – Allen Macaulay - The Record – January 16, 1994

The Ski Industry – New Jersey Business – November 1974

Vernon Township Historical Society – Highland Lakes, NJ

HIDDEN VALLEY SKI AREA

Don & Bonnie Begraft
    Owners of Hidden Valley – personal interviews

Hidden Valley ski area brochures

Hidden Valley ski area - website

John Pier – Former owner – personal interview

Jeff Pier – New Jersey Ski Racing Association – personal interview

Skiing The Hills Of Home – Thrills In Your Own Back Yard
    By: Allen Macaulay – The Record – January 16, 1994

HIGH POINT STATE PARK

Erie Snow Trains
    brochure – 1936

High Point Lodge Opens for Guests Staying Overnight
    Newark Sunday Call – 4/4/1937

High Point Of The Blue Mountains
    By: Ronald J. Dupont, Jr. & Kevin Wright (1990)
    Sussex County Historical Society

High Point Park Impresses Group
    New York Times – 12/28/1936

HIGH POINT SKI STATE PARK

High Point State Park And The Civilian Conservation Corps
    By Peter Osborne (2002)

John Keator
    Superintendent – High Point State Park

Many ski areas 'lost' in Sussex County – Jennie Sweetman with Liz Holste
    New Jersey Sunday Herald – March 9, 2003

Montague Association for Restoration of Community History (M.A.R.C.H.)

Myra Snook
    Friends Of High Point State Park

New Jersey Ski Areas – New Jersey Department of Conservation (1964)

Ski Expert At Park
    Sussex Independent – 3/18/1937

Skiers & Skaters to Find High Point Park a Paradise
    Newark Evening News – 11/27/1936

Skiers to Find High Point a Paradise
    Newark Evening News – 11/27/1936

Sno' Time To Jump
    Newark Evening News – 12/31/1936

Where To Ski – Ski Guide To the U.S. and Canada – John & David Landman 1949

World Ski Book – Edited by Frank Elkins & Frank Harper – 1949

HOLIDAY LAKE (High Point Country Club)

Alicia Batko – Montague Association For Restoration Of Community History

Holiday Lake Inc. – brochure

Many ski areas 'lost' in Sussex County – Jennie Sweetman with Liz Holste
    New Jersey Sunday Herald – March 9, 2003

Fred Merusi – phone interview (3/17/03)

New Jersey Ski Areas – New Jersey Department of Conservation (1968)

Town Blocks Child Invasion
    World Journal Tribune – 10/2/1966

HOLLY MOUNTAIN

Holly Mountain – brochure – 1979/1980 season

Lower Alloways Creek Township Municipal Office

New Jersey Ski Areas – New Jersey Department of Conservation (1973)

Salem County Chamber Of Commerce

Salem County Historical Society

The Ski Industry – New Jersey Business – November 1974

HOLMDEL SKI AREA

Holmdel Park - brochure

New Jersey Ski Areas – New Jersey Department of Conservation (1964)

New Jersey Ski Areas – New Jersey Department of Conservation (1968)

JUGTOWN MOUNTAIN

County's First Commercial Ski Area Is Almost Ready
    Hunterdon Democrat – 12/28/1961

Down Skiing Trails
    by Tom Evans - The Courier News – 1/4/1962

It Was All Downhill At Jugtown Mountain Ski Area
    Hunterdon Democrat Observer – 2/22/1988

Jugtown Slope Being Prepared For Best Ski Area In State
    Hunterdon Democrat Newspaper

Jugtown Slope Is Aided By Mercury
The Democrat – 1/4/1962

Doug Kiovsky - Hunterdon County Parks Department

New Jersey Ski Areas – New Jersey Department of Conservation (1964)

Prosperity On The Down Slopes – New Jersey Business – January 1967

Frank Vones – operator of Jugtown Mountain Ski Area

LAKE TELEMARK SKI JUMPS

Growing Up In Bay Ridge and Lake Telemark
   by Walter Swanson

Lake Telemark: Cradle Of XC in North Jersey?
   by Peter Minde - XC Ski NJ

Lake Telemark Ski Jump – Oddfrid Tokle
   Rockaway Township 1976 Bicentennial Quilt

Ellie Mason – Rockaway Township Library

Art Tokle, Jr. – Chairman Eastern USSA Ski Jumping Association

Richard & Ellen Tonnesen – personal interviews March 2003

MADISON SQUARE GARDEN SKI SHOWS

Battle of Fifth Avenue – Skiing Heritage – March 2003

Come in and Ski for yourself
   Wanamaker's ad - New York Times – 12/28/1936

Winter Carnival Draws 13,000 Fans To Final Session
   New York Times – 12/13/1936

MORGAN FARM SKI HILL

Essex County Historical Society

MOUNT BETHEL

New Jersey Ski Areas – New Jersey Department of Conservation (1968)

New Jersey Ski Areas – New Jersey Division of Economic Development (1972)

New Jersey Ski Areas – New Jersey Department of Conservation (1973)

The Ski Industry – New Jersey Business – November 1974

Township of Mansfield Municipal Office

Warren County Historical Society – Debra Natyzak

MIGHTY MOUNT MUNSTERER

Bill Bolte – personal interview

Jerry Munsterer – personal interview

Roy Scovill – phone interview

Ski Dads – Becky Munsterer – Ski Magazine – May/June 2002

MOUNTAIN CREEK

Mountain Creek – brochures

mountaincreek.com (website)

Our ride with Kass
 Advertiser – North Jersey – 3/14/2002

Resort will stay course after fire
 The Star Ledger – 10/12/1999

Ski resort owners vow new lodge in 2 months
 The Star Ledger – 10/22/1999
Vernon cops, State Police differ on fire at ski lodge
 The Star Ledger – 10/13/1999

NEWTON SKI TOW

Alicia Batko - Montague Association For Restoration Of Community History

Hill Echoes – Watchung Ski Club

Many ski areas 'lost' in Sussex County – Jennie Sweetman w/Liz Holste
 New Jersey Sunday Herald – March 9, 2003

Where To Ski – Ski Guide to the U.S. and Canada – Joan & David Landman -1949

Clarence Wyker - owner – personal interview

NORTH JERSEY COUNTRY CLUB SKI JUMPS

Swedish Ski Club - website

Margaretta Ugander – personal interview

PEAPACK

Melvyn Blaufuss - owner

Hill Echoes – Watchung Ski Club – Erling Omland

New Jersey Ski Areas – New Jersey Department of Conservation (1964)

New Jersey Ski Areas – New Jersey Department of Conservation (1968)

New Jersey Ski Areas – New Jersey Division of Economic Development (1972)

New Jersey Ski Areas – New Jersey Department of Conservation (1973)

New Peapack Ski Tow Draws Hundred Of Winter Sports Enthusiasts To County – 1940

Remember when there was skiing in Peapack?
   by: Marc O'Reilly
   Hills-Bedminster Press 12/20/1995

The Ski Industry – New Jersey Business – November 1974

Ski Peapack – brochure

Skiing Bonanza photo – Newark Evening News

The Little Ski Area That Could
   by Larry Bataille

World Ski Book – edited by Frank Elkins & Frank Harper - 1949

PINE NEEDLE SLOPE

Competition – James M. Spees – Watchung Ski Club

Arnie Kirbach, Sr. – personal interview - October 12, 2002

Leaves From A Skier's Journal - Skiing The Pine Needles
   by Erling Omland – Mountain Times 8/23/2001

Many ski areas 'lost' in Sussex County – Jennie Sweetman with Liz Holste
   New Jersey Sunday Herald – March 9, 2003

Needles And Skis – by Ken Littlefield
   The Ski Bulletin – November 1940

Erling Omland – phone interview – January 25, 2003

Quick, Watson, The Needles – by Oscar E. Naumann
   The Ski Bulletin – November 1939

Skiing on Pine Needles – Newark News – October 1939

PLAYBOY CLUB HOTEL

Playboy Club News - 1965

Playboy/Great Gorge Resort & Country Club
1974 brochure

Playboy Club and Golf Course Are Nearing Completion
Herald News – 6/6/71

Nearing Completion
North Jersey Photo News – 7/15/71

Vernon Hotel gets new name; conference resort plan unveiled
by: Gary Kleelblatt – Herald News – 8/24/89

ROCK VIEW HOTEL

Erie Snow Trains brochure

Rock View Hotel brochures

Alicia Batko – Montague Association For Restoration of Community History

ROCCO'S VILLA SUNSET

World Ski Book – edited by Frank Elkins & Frank Harper - 1949

SKI/ACTION MOUNTAIN

Emil DelConte
Owner – phone interview

McMogul Wintertime, And The Schussing Is Easy
By: Michael Bamberger – Philadelphia Inquirer 12/24/89

New Jersey Ski Areas – New Jersey Department of Conservation (1968)

New Jersey Ski Areas – New Jersey Division of Economic Development (1972)

New Jersey Ski Areas – New Jersey Department of Conservation (1973)

Planners permit lot expansion at Pine Hill park
by John McDonough – Courier-Post – 6/5/84

Prosperity On The Down Slopes – New Jersey Business – January 1967

Skiing Under the stars in Pine Hill
by Karen Kennedy-Hall - Courier-Post – 10/10/95

SKI/ACTION MOUNTAIN

The Ski Industry – New Jersey Business – November 1974

A Winter Holiday In South Jersey
    The Evening Bulletin – 2/3/78

SKI TRAINS

Erie Snow Trains – brochure 1939

Erie Snow Trains – brochure 1950s

New York Times – various articles 1930s/1940s

Rail Notes: Snow Trips – New York Times – December 26, 1937

When Snow-Clad Hills Call
    by John Kieran - New York Times – 1/13/1936

SNOW BOWL

Jefferson Township Public Library

Mahlon Dickerson Reservation Trail Map
    Morris County Parks Commission

Morris County Parks & Recreation Commission

New Jersey Ski Areas – New Jersey Department of Conservation (1964)

New Jersey Ski Areas – New Jersey Department of Conservation (1968)

New Jersey Ski Areas – New Jersey Division of Economic Development (1972)
New Jersey Ski Areas – New Jersey Department of Conservation (1973)

Proposed Capital Budget At $30 million
    by: James A. Duffy - Daily Record – 11/14/1999

Prosperity On The Down Slopes – New Jersey Business – January 1967

Joe Riggs – phone interview – January 2003

Roy Scovill – phone interview - February 3, 2003

Snow Bowl – advertisements – Star-Ledger newspaper

Snow Bowl Ski Area – contour map
    Jerrald L. Karlan – Architect 9/1972

The Ski Industry – New Jersey Business – November 1974

SUCCASUNNA SKI AREA

Hill Echoes – Watchung Ski Club

Erling Omland – Watchung Ski Club

World Ski Book – edited by Frank Elkins & Frank Harper - 1949

SUSSEX SKI TOW

Alicia Batko - Montague Association for Restoration of Community History

Hill Echoes –Erling Omland / Watchung Ski Club

Many ski areas 'lost' in Sussex County – Jennie Sweetman with Liz Holste
    New Jersey Sunday Herald – March 9, 2003

Where To Ski – Ski Guide to the U.S. and Canada – Joan & David Landman - 1949

World Ski Book – edited by Frank Elkins & Frank Harper – 1949

THOMPSON PARK SKI VILLAGE

Jamesburg Library

Middlesex County Parks Department

Monroe Township Historic Commission

New Jersey Ski Areas – New Jersey Department of Conservation (1968)

New Jersey Ski Areas – New Jersey Division of Economic Development (1972)

New Jersey Ski Areas – New Jersey Department of Conservation (1973)

The Ski Industry – New Jersey Business – November 1974

THUNDER MOUNTAIN / EAGLE MOUNTAIN

Claude Ballester – National Ski Patrol – personal interview

History of Ringwood
    Borough of Ringwood Chamber of Commerce

New $2.5 million lodge to open
    Argus – 3/14/1982

New Jersey Ski Areas – New Jersey Department of Conservation (1964)

THUNDER MOUNTAIN

Park's new $2 million rec facility nears completion
    Argus – 9/6/1981

Shepherd Lake Recreation Beginning To Pay Off
    By: George J. Fitzmaurice – Herald News 1970

Shepherd Lake Shopping Center?
    Argus – 1/25/1981

State Park Service – Ringwood State Park – 3/19/2002

VERNON SKI TOW

About The Vernon Ski Tow
    by: Edward Hine – November 2002

Many ski areas 'lost' in Sussex County – Jennie Sweetman with Liz Holste
    New Jersey Sunday Herald – March 9, 2003

Vernon Ski Tow – promo sheet – January 1948

Vernon Ski Tow – promo sheet - 1949

Woody Walker – personal interview – January 2003
    Ski Patrol – Vernon Ski Tow

Where To Ski – Ski Guide to the U.S. and Canada – Joan & David Landman - 1949

World Ski Book – edited by Frank Elkins & Frank Harper - 1949

VERNON VALLEY SKI AREA

Canoe Races held at Vernon
    Photo News – 3/18/71

New Jersey Ski Areas – New Jersey Division of Economic Development (1972)

New Jersey Ski Areas – New Jersey Department of Conservation (1973)

Snowy slopes beckoning skiers – Special events to mark 25th season at Vernon Valley-Great Gorge
    by: Sharon Sheridan – The New Jersey Herald – 12/22/89

Sussex County Library (Dorothy Henry Branch) - Vernon, NJ

Sussex County Library (Main Branch) – Frankford Twp., NJ

The Ski Industry – New Jersey Business – November 1974

VERNON VALLEY SKI AREA

Vernon 2000
    by Ron Dupont, Jr.

Vernon Township Historical Society – Highland Lakes, NJ

Vernon Valley/Great Gorge - brochures

CUBCO BINDING COMPANY

American Ski Journal – ads

Cubco Bindings – The British Ski Book For 1958

Mitch Cubberly – nomination paper to National Ski Hall Of Fame
    by: Joseph Powers
    From New England Ski Museum files

INDOOR SKI SLIDES

Battle of Fifth Avenue – Skiing Heritage – March 2003

"Dry Skiing" Lures Many – (Borax Covered Slides Are Effective as Substitutes for Snowy Slopes)
    By: John Markland – New York Times – December 13, 1936

Newark Evening News – various articles

New York Times – various articles

Skiing on a 'Magic Carpet' – Newark Evening News

DANNY KASS

Star-Ledger newspaper

U.S. SKI TEAM website

NEW JERSEY SKI COUNCIL

Join N.J. Council ... and see the world
    Skiing Plus – Star-Ledger – January 13, 2000

New Jersey Ski Council website

New Jersey State Race – Newark News (1942)

NEW JERSEY SKI RACING ASSOCIATION

New Jersey Ski Racing Association – Competition Guide 2003

John Pier – Former President
Jeff Pier – Current President

10th MOUNTAIN DIVISION

Arnie Kirbach, Sr. – personal interview

Erling Omland – phone interview

10th Mountain Division website

DONNA WEINBRECHT

Donna Weinbrecht –personal interview

Donna Weinbrecht's Comeback - Ski Magazine – February 2001

Gold Rush – Sports Illustrated For Kids – February 1992

Jersey ski champ takes gold in her 'most beautiful victory' – Star Ledger – February 14, 1992

Skiing The Hills Of Home – Thrills In Your Own Back Yard
  By: Allen Macaulay – The Record – January 16, 1994

U.S. Freestyle Team – Donna Weinbrecht bio
  Skiing Magazine – Winter 2001/2002

U.S. National Ski Hall of Fame – Ishpeming, MI

U.S. SKI TEAM website

OTHER REFERENCES

Bill Bolte – personal interview

U.S. National Ski Hall Of Fame Museum, Inc. – Ishpeming, MI

New England Ski Museum – Franconia, NH

U.S. Ski & Snowboard Association – Park City, UT

Jerry Munsterer – phone interview

Doug Kiovsky – Hunterdon County Department of Parks and Recreation

OTHER REFERENCES

New Jersey's Outdoor Guide 1989
    by: New Jersey Division Travel & Tourism

A Short History Of Alpine Skiing – From Telemark to Today
    by: Morten Lund
    (Skiing Heritage – A Ski History Quarterly
    Winter 1996 – Volume 8, No. 1)

New Jersey Ski Council – Skiers Guides (various years)

Westview Geographies of the United States – New Jersey
    by: Charles A. Stansfield

Peaks of excitement – Star-Ledger – June 20, 2003

Ski New Jersey (1972 brochure)
    New Jersey Commerce & Economic Growth Commission
    Trenton, New Jersey

Ski & discover the Jersey (1973 brochure)
    Division of Economic Development – Trenton, New Jersey

Skiing in New Jersey – From The 1920's to 1977
    By: Janet Bamford – New Jersey Outdoors – Jan/Feb 1977

Skiing in New Jersey
    by: Ruth Kattermann
    Chapter in Travelling New Jersey by: Frank Esposito 1978

Skiing Information – New York Times – December 25, 1936

The White Book Of Ski Areas United States and Canada
    By: Inter-Ski Services, Inc. - 1976

The White Book Of Ski Areas United States and Canada
    by: Inter-Ski Services, Inc. – 1989

Skiing: New Jersey's Got It
    by Brian Eck – Daily Record – January 1, 1982

Skiing? Get A Lift From The Slopes Of Jersey
    by: Roger Farrell - Daily Record – January 9, 1981

Pursing Powder On Slope And Trail
    by: Helen Lippman Collins & Patricia Reardon
    New York Times – 1/10/88

Watchung At Fifty (April 29, 1988)
    Watchung The Early Years A Reading By Erling Omland
    by: Erling Omland – Watchung Ski Club

OTHER REFERENCES

History Of the Swedish Ski Club
       by: Lars Radberg – 10/1/93
       Swedish Ski Club 70th Anniversary Dinner

Away We Go!
       edited by: Michaela M. Mole – Fourth Edition – © 1976

Discovering New Jersey
       by: Thomas R. Radko
       © 1982 by Rutgers - The State University Of New Jersey

The WPA Guide To 1930's New Jersey
New Jersey – Outdoor Guide
       by: New Jersey Division of Travel And Tourism

Gary Brooks – National Ski Patrol – New Jersey

Claude Ballester – National Ski Patrol – New Jersey

Arnie Kirbach, Sr. – (pine needle slope skiing & 10th Mountain Division) – personal interview

Vermont Ski Museum – Stowe, VT

Woodstock Historical Society
       Woodstock, VT

The Ski Tow Turns Fifty
       by: Millyn Moore
       Vermont Life Magazine – Winter 1983

New England Skiing
       by: E. John B. Allen – 1997

"Dry Skiing" Lures Many
       by: John Markland
       New York Times – 12/13/1936

'Snow' Makes City Winter Festival
       by: David Halberstam – New York Times – 11/28/1960

New Trails Abound For Skiers
       by: Frank Elkins - New York Times – 12/6/1936

LIBRARIES

Kinnelon Public Library – Kinnelon, NJ
Jefferson Township Public Library – Milton, NJ
Mahwah Public Library – Mahwah, NJ
Morris County Public Library – Whippany, NJ
New Jersey State Library – Trenton, NJ
Newark Public Library – Newark, NJ
Peapack Library – Peapack, NJ
Ringwood Public Library – Ringwood, NJ
Rockaway Township Library – Rockaway, NJ
Sussex County Library – Dorothy Henry Branch – Vernon, NJ
Sussex County Library – Main Branch – Frankford, NJ
Wayne Public Library – Wayne, NJ
West Milford Library – West Milford, NJ

About The Author

Elizabeth Holste was born in Ridgewood, New York in 1960. Both sets of her grandparents owned bungalows in Highland Lakes near Vernon. Because of that she was able to spend many summers and winters in the mountains of New Jersey while growing up. In 1973 she moved to Kinnelon with her parents and her sister.

Skiing is her favorite sport. Some people laughed at her when she told them she learned how to ski in New Jersey. They didn't believe that the state had any ski areas. This book is proof that there was and still is skiing in New Jersey. Skiing In New Jersey? is a book for all ages.

Elizabeth's first ski hills were the snow covered roads of Highland Lakes. After conquering the hills of Highland Lakes, she went on to the slopes of the Craigmeur and Great Gorge ski areas. She is a member of the High Life Ski Club - one of New Jersey's largest ski clubs. During the winter she skis at the few New Jersey ski areas that are still open and at many of the northeastern resorts. She also gets to some of the western ski slopes as well.

Elizabeth has a Business degree with a minor in Marketing. During her career she has worked for various publishing companies and national magazine distributors. For several years she also worked in the field of television advertising.

Her love of skiing is what inspired her to write this book. The adventure into New Jersey's ski history began when she and some of her friends were talking about what slopes they skied while growing up skiing. To her surprise she found out about some old New Jersey ski hills that she never knew about. Skiing In New Jersey? is the culmination of the adventure that Elizabeth had while researching the history of skiing in the state.

Printed in the United States
84143LV00003B/67/A